G000048902

# C
# Pocket Book

# C
# Pocket Book

**Conor Sexton**

Newnes
An imprint of Butterworth-Heinemann Ltd
Linacre House, Jordan Hill, Oxford OX2 8DP

℞ A member of the Reed Elsevier plc group

OXFORD LONDON BOSTON
MUNICH NEW DELHI SINGAPORE SYDNEY
TOKYO TORONTO WELLINGTON

First published 1991
Reprinted 1993, 1994

**British Library Cataloguing in Publication Data**
Sexton, Conor
    Newnes C pocket book.
    I. Title
    005.13

ISBN 0 7506 0221 X

Produced by Butford Technical Publishing
Butford Farm, Bodenham, Hereford
Printed and bound in Great Britain
by Clays Ltd, St Ives plc

# Contents

For Siobhan

# Preface

Since it first appeared in 1978, the C programming language has become a language of choice for software developers working in many different application areas. It is now widely used by hundreds of thousands of programmers and by students in very many educational establishments. Many popular software packages, database systems and software development environments are themselves written in C.

C is particularly suitable for system programming and applications in communications and graphics software. The C language is by no means limited to use in these fields; it is probably the most versatile of all programming languages and may be used for almost any conceivable application.

C originated with the Unix operating system, but has since been moved ('ported') to computer systems of all sizes, using diverse operating systems.

### The 'mid-level' language

Although it has many of the characteristics of conventional high-level third-generation programming languages, C is accurately called 'mid-level' because of its ability to mimic the constructs employed in widely-used assembler languages. Much code – particularly operating-system code – which has traditionally been written using assembler languages, may instead be developed using C, with concomitant savings in development time and incidence of errors.

C is often considered a high-level language because it incorporates the block-structured approach to the construction of programs, has iterative and conditional statements similar to those in Pascal, PL/1 and ALGOL, and has a reasonable level of data-type checking.

C does not, however, contain any 'built-in functions' of the conventional type used for such things as string operations, file access and mathematical calculation. All functions outside the strict grammatical definition of the language itself are defined in external libraries and included in the C program source code.

C is thus a small language compared to the high-level languages. Compilers for C are also small and relatively easy to implement. Standardisation of C's syntax and of a subset of libraries has resulted in the language being implemented on computer systems of all types from personal computers to the most powerful of supercomputers. Extreme portability of software written in C has resulted, with a consequent increase in its worldwide usage.

Many constructs in C are similar to those used in typical assemblers. This is particularly evident in the case of C's use of pointers to data items, which closely mimics assembler address indirection. One result is that it is possible to implement operating systems and device drivers in C, with little or no use of assembler, even at the lowest level of the software-machine interface.

### The ANSI standard

C was first implemented under the Unix operating system by Dennis Ritchie in the early 1970s. In 1973, Unix was itself rewritten, largely in C. The language was loosely standardised in Kernighan and Ritchie's 'The C Programming Language' of 1978. In 1989, C was formally defined and standardised by the American National Standards Institute (ANSI) X3J11 committee.

This standard has gained remarkable acceptance in the user community. As a result, C is one of the few computer languages which has one standard definition, yet is not associated exclusively with a single supplier. Therefore, C programs adhering to the ANSI standard may be readily moved between different computer environments and can be expected to work correctly without modification. The popularity and applicability of C have increased accordingly.

**About this book**

This book covers, in as succinct a manner as possible, the whole definition of the C language with the exception of a few of the more obscure details: for example, trigraph sequences and nesting of the preprocessor token-merging operator are not dealt with. It is intended to be readable, yet terse and unambiguous; short yet comprehensive. The first chapter conducts the reader on a 'tour' of C; at the end of the chapter, the reader has addressed most important aspects of the language and should be in a position to write non-trivial C programs.

Subsequent chapters treat the topics raised in the first in detail and present a number of tested illustrative examples. At the end of each chapter a number of small programs and code fragments are given which contain deliberately-inserted syntactic and semantic errors. The reader is invited to find the errors, which are pointed out elsewhere in the text.

Chapter 2 explains C data representation and storage. Chapter 3 treats the definition and use of functions in C and the consequent organisation and structure of C programs. Chapter 4 defines the rules relating to expressions and the precedence and associativity of their operators. Chapter 5 defines C's control-flow constructs.

Chapters 6 and 7 explain all aspects of arrays and structures, giving preliminary information on their use with pointers. Chapter 8 goes into pointers in detail and is particularly important, pointers being the area which sets C apart from all other languages. Chapter 9 is concerned with file I/O and library functions. Chapter 10 deals with remaining features of the C language.

Experienced programmers of high-level languages may be able to read quickly over the first five chapters, which treat areas of C that are not fundamentally different to such languages. The remaining chapters should be read with care; in its treatment of pointers, especially, C is unique.

This book only covers the 'common subset' of C as defined by the ANSI standard. It is generic and applies to all environments using the standard. It does not deal with graphics or other libraries specific to particular computing environments or with implementation-dependent extensions to the C language.

The book should be useful as an introductory text for novice programmers and as an accessible reference for experienced software developers.

**Conor Sexton**

# 1 A Tour of C

## 1.1 Compilation and execution

A C program is a set of one or more functions and data, known as *source code*, 'written' by the programmer with an editor program. The source code is stored in a file with an arbitrary name, by convention followed by the suffix '.c'.

To render the C program intelligible to and executable by the computer and operating system, the source code must be processed in a number of steps.

Firstly, the C program source code is scanned by the C *preprocessor*. The preprocessor carries out necessary text substitutions on the source code and causes inclusion of optional 'header files' into the source code. The operation of the preprocessor is explained in Chapter 10. The changed source code is then passed to the compiler.

The *compiler* is itself a program which, according to the grammatical rules of the C language, parses and analyses the source code into an intermediate form known as *object code*.

On many systems, the name of the object code file is the same as that of the source code file, except that it is suffixed with '.o' or '.obj' instead of '.c'.

Next, the *linkage editor*, or *loader*, combines the object code with the object code of library files and the run-time system. Variable references are resolved and an executable program file for the 'target' computer and operating system is produced.

The executable program file may then be run on the computer.

Depending on the system being used, the compile and load steps may be carried out in what appears to the user as one step. Compiler and loader options are always available to control this sequence.

## 1.2   Simple C programs

The following is the minimal C program:

```
main ()
{
}
```

Every C program must consist of one or more functions. The code shown above is a function. The
function name is 'main'. Every C program must
have one (and only one) 'main' function.

The parentheses '()' enclose the names of
parameters which may be supplied to the function.
There are no parameter names here, but the rules
for inclusion of these are given in Chapter 3.

The curly braces '{}' are a compound statement: in
fact a *null* compound statement because they do
not contain any statements.

On execution, the program, as might be expected,
does nothing.

The following program is slightly more meaningful:

```
main ()
{
    printf ("Hello World\n");
}
```

'printf' is a call to a library function. It is *not* part of
the C language itself. The 'printf' line is nonetheless a statement, which is (and must be) terminated
by a semicolon. The text within the parentheses is
an argument to the called library function 'printf'.

Executing this program causes the string

```
Hello World
```

to appear on your standard output device, which is
probably a terminal. The '\n', C's way of specifying
advance to a new line, causes the output to advance one line after the text is displayed.

Using your editor, type in this program and call it
'greeting.c'. Then compile and load it.

## 1.3  Functions

'main', as shown in the previous section, is a special function: it must be present in every C program.

A C program may – and usually does – contain an arbitrary number of programmer-defined functions. The following is a simple general form for all functions:

```
<functionname>()
{
    <statements>
}
```

Here is a C program containing two functions:

```
/* Two-function program */
main ()
{
    printf ("Hello World\n");
    myfunc ();
}
myfunc ()
{
    printf ("Hello World again\n");
}
/* End of program text */
```

In this program, 'main' contains two statements: first the 'printf' we have already seen; second a call to the function 'myfunc', which contains a further, slightly different, 'printf' statement.

Again, enter this program and compile and load it. The displayed result on execution should be:

```
Hello World
Hello World again
```

The statement

```
myfunc();
```

is the call from 'main' to the function 'myfunc'.

On execution, control is passed to 'myfunc' from 'main'. When the single statement in 'myfunc' has been executed, control is returned to the first statement in 'main' after the function call. Because, in this case, the function call is the last statement in 'main', the whole program immediately stops execution.

Note that the function call is a statement and must be terminated with a semi-colon; the header of the called function is not a statement and must not be appended with a semi-colon.

Comments are included in the program between the '/*' and '*/' delimiters.

The text of comments has no effect at all on the execution of the program. The compiler ignores comments and does not generate object code for them.

Syntax errors with comments can have serious effects. If the trailing '*/' is left out, the compiler will keep on searching for it until the end of the program and the compilation process will fail.

If the characters in '/*' or '*/' are separated by one or more spaces (e.g. '/ *') the compiler will not recognise the text between them as comments. The comment delimiters are pairs of characters.

Comments must not be nested:

```
/* Comment text /* nested */ in error */
```

the first '*/' will end the comment, and the compiler will try to process 'in error */'.

## 1.4   Simple data representation

*Variables* in C are data objects that may change in value. A variable is given a name by means of a definition, which allocates storage space for the data and associates the storage location with the variable name.

The C language defines four fundamental representations of data:

integer
character
floating-point
double floating-point

Each of these is associated with a special type specifier:

| **int** | specifies an integer variable |
| **char** | specifies a character variable |
| **float** | specifies a fractional-number variable |
| **double** | specifies a fractional-number variable with more decimal places |

Any of the type specifiers may be 'qualified' with the type qualifier 'const', which specifies that the variable must not be changed after it is initialised.

A data definition is of the following general form:

```
<type-specifier> <name>;
```

A variable name is also called an *identifier*.

The following are some examples of simple data definitions in C:

```
int    goals;   /* integer variable */
char   c;       /* variable holding char-
                   acter value eg: 'b' */
float  balance; /* variable holding bank
                   balance */
const double  x; /* invariant high-
                    precision variable */
```

## 1.5   Operators

C has a full set of arithmetic, relational and logical *operators*. It also has some interesting operators for direct bit-level manipulation of data objects. This is another of C's likenesses to assembler.

The binary arithmetic operators in C are:

| + | addition |
| - | subtraction |

| * | multiplication |
| / | division |
| % | modulus |

There is no operator for exponentiation; in line with general C practice, this is implemented as a special function in an external library.

Both + and - may be used as unary operators, as in the cases of -5 and +8. There is no difference between +8 and 8; for completeness, the unary plus operator has been implemented in the ANSI C standard.

The modulus operator, '%', provides a useful 'remainder' facility:

```
17%4  /* gives 1, the remainder after
          division */
```

The assignment operator '=' assigns a value to a memory location associated with a variable name. For example:

```
a = 7;
pi = 3.1415927;
```

Relational operators in C are:

| < | less than |
| > | greater than |
| >= | greater than or equal to |
| <= | less than or equal to |
| != | not equal |
| == | test for equality |

Care is needed in use of the equality test '=='. A beginning programmer will at least once make the mistake of using a single '=' as an equality test; experienced programmers do it all the time!

To write:

```
x = 5;
```

is to assign the value 5 to the memory location associated with the name x.

x == 5, on the other hand, tests the value at the memory location associated with the name x for equality with 5.

Confusion here can result in grave program logic errors. It is a good idea, with the editor, to check all usages in the source code of '=' and '==' manually. The compiler will not catch these mistakes for you.

Logical operators provided by C are:

| && | AND |
| II | OR |
| ! | NOT (unary negation operator) |

If two variables are defined as follows:

```
int    x;
int    y;
/* initialise x and y */
x = 4;
y = 5;
```

then

```
(x == 4) && (y == 5)    is TRUE
(x == 4) || (y == 3)    is TRUE
!x                      is FALSE
```

As described in Chapter 4, any non-zero variable is inherently TRUE; its negation is therefore FALSE.

Chapter 4 also deals with bit-level logical operators.

## 1.6    Expressions and statements

An *expression* is any valid combination of function names, variables, constants, operators and sub-expressions. A simple statement is an expression terminated by a semi-colon.

The following are all expressions:

```
a = 5
printf ("Hello World\n")
a = b + c
a = b + (c * d)
```

Every expression has a type, depending on the types of its constituents, and a boolean value. These facts are explained in full in Chapter 4.

An expression may be assigned to a variable:

```
a = printf ("Hello World\n");
```

In this statement, a is assigned the value returned by the library function 'printf' – the number of characters output by 'printf'. More usefully:

```
a = b + c;
```

assigns to a the sum of the values of variables b and c.

Expressions in C may be extremely complex. Here is a slightly less simple one:

```
a = b + c * d
```

In this case, the order of arithmetic evaluation is important.

```
a = b + (c * d)
```

is not the same as

```
a = (b + c) * d
```

because the precedence of the operators is different. The full rules of precedence and associativity are given in Chapter 4.

For the moment, we can summarise the order of precedence with a subset of C's operators:

| | |
|---|---|
| () | Sub-expressions surrounded with parentheses (these are of the highest precedence and are evaluated first) |
| ! - | The unary negation operator and unary minus |
| * / % | The arithmetic operators |
| + - | The plus and minus binary arithmetic operators |
| < <= > >= | The relational operators |
| != == | The equality operators |
| && \|\| | The logical operators (which are of low precedence) |

Statements may optionally be grouped inside pairs of curly braces '{}'. One or more statements so grouped form a compound statement.

## 1.7   Standard device I/O

The concept of 'standard device' is important in C. If you are using a terminal, you may think of the standard input as being the keyboard and the standard output as the screen.

A C program may read text from the standard input by means of the 'getchar' library function and send text to the standard output using 'printf', which we have already seen, or the 'putchar' library function.

There are several other methods of Input/Output, described in Chapter 9.

'printf' is the name of a library function. Its declaration is stored in the header file 'stdio.h'. The '.h' suffix is a convention used to denote a header file. Header files are included in C programs by means of the '#include' directive, as follows:

```
#include "stdio.h"
```

'stdio.h' contains many declarations of library functions, such as 'printf', as well as other useful definitions, including those for NULL (binary zero) and EOF (end-of-file, usually represented as -1).

The 'printf' function call includes at least one argument. The first argument is always a string and is called the *format string*.

The format string contains two kinds of objects: ordinary characters, which are copied to the standard output device, and format codes, which are prefixed by a '%'. The format string causes 'printf' to output the following arguments according to the formats.

If they are specified, the second and subsequent arguments to 'printf' are variables or expressions.

Here is an example:

```
#include "stdio.h"
```

```
main()
{
    int       num;
    float     e;

    num       = 6;
    e         = 2.718282;

    printf ("Number is %d, fraction is
                        %f\n", num,e);
}
```

The 'printf' call causes the following output:

```
Number is 6, fraction is 2.718282
```

Type in this program, compile it and verify the result.

Fundamental 'printf' format codes are:

| | |
|---|---|
| %d | decimal integer |
| %f | floating-point number |
| %g | double floating-point number |
| %s | string |
| %c | character |

With these codes, and variations on them, very sophisticated output can be generated using 'printf'.

The 'getchar' function reads the next input character from the standard input device and returns that character as its value.

Consider the following code segment:

```
int c;

c = getchar();
```

After its execution, c contains the next character read from the standard input. The statement:

```
putchar(c);
```

writes the character represented by the value stored at c to the standard output device.

## 1.8  Conditional statements

The 'if' statement is used to allow decisions to be made by the program logic.

The following is the general form of 'if':

```
if (<expression>)
    <statement1>
else
    <statement2>
```

The 'else' part is optional: an 'if' statement with one or more subject statements and no alternative provided by 'else' is legal. For example:

```
if (nobufs < MAXBUF)
    nobufs = nobufs + 1;
```

Here, if the number of buffers used is less than the allowed maximum, the counter of used buffers is incremented by one.

Two or more statements may be made subject to an 'if' by use of a compound statement:

```
if (day == 1)
    {
    printf ("Monday\n");
    week = week + 1;
    }
if (day == 2)
    {
    printf ("Tuesday\n");
    run_sales_report();
    }
```

'else' should be used where the program logic suggests it.

```
if (day == 1)
    {
    printf ("Monday\n");
    week = week + 1;
    }
else
if (day == 2)
    {
```

```
    printf ("Tuesday\n");
    run_sales_report();
    }
```

Use of 'else' here stops execution of the 'Tuesday'
code if the value of day is 1.

It is possible to nest 'if' statements:

```
if (month == 2)
    if (day == 29)
        printf ("Leap Year!!\n");
    else
        printf ("February\n");
```

Chapter 5 gives all the rules for use of 'if' and 'else'.

## 1.9   Iteration

Where the 'if' statement allows a branch in the program flow of control, the 'for', 'while' and 'do'
statements allow repeated execution of code in
'loops'.

```
#include "stdio.h"

main()
{
    int x;

    x = 1;
    while (x < 100)
        {
        printf ("Number %d\n",x);
        x = x + 1;
        }
}
```

This program prints all the numbers from 1 to 99
inclusive.

```
#include "stdio.h"

main()
{
    int x;

    for (x = 1; x < 100; x = x + 1)
```

```
        printf ("Number %d\n",x);
}
```

This program does exactly the same. Try testing either or both of these programs.

The 'for' statement is often used when the condition limits – in this case 1 and 100 – are known in advance.

The general form of the 'for' statement is as follows:

```
for (<expr1>;<expr2>;<expr3>)
    <statement>
```

Any of the expressions may be omitted, but the two semicolons must be included. For example:

```
for (;;)
```

results in an infinite loop.

The 'do' statement is a special case of 'while'. It is generally used where is it is required to execute the loop statements at least once:

```
do
    {
    c = getchar();
    if (c == EOF)
        printf ("End of text\n");
    else
        /* do something with  c  */
    } while (c != EOF);
```

The symbolic constant 'EOF' is defined in 'stdio.h' as the numeric value -1. The keystroke sequence required to generate this value is system-dependent. On Unix systems, 'EOF' is generated by **Ctrl-D**; on PCs by **Ctrl-Z**.

Use of 'do' instead of 'while' is relatively rare: perhaps 5% of all cases.

The following example illustrates use of 'putchar', 'getchar', 'if' and one of the iterative statements.

```
/* Program to copy standard input to
   standard output but stripping out
   newlines    */

#include "stdio.h"
```

```
main()
{
    int c;

    while ((c = getchar()) != EOF)
        {
        if (c != '\n')
            putchar(c);
        }
}
```

Notice the 'getchar' function call embedded in the 'while' condition expression. This is legal and also considered good practice in concise programming.

## 1.10 Arrays

Any of the data objects we have seen may be stored and represented as an *array*, which is an aggregate data object.

An array of ten integer variables may be defined as follows:

```
int    num[10];
```

In general, an array is a collection of data objects of the same type.

The value within the square brackets '[]' is known as a *subscript*. In the case above, ten contiguous memory locations for integer values are allocated by the compiler. In C, the subscript range is from zero to 9.

When using a variable as a subscript, care must be taken to count from zero and stop one short of the subscript value. Failure to do this will result in unpleasant program errors.

The following is a simple example of use of arrays:

```
/* Fill integer array with zeros, fill
   character array with blanks*/

#include "stdio.h"

main()
```

```
{
    int    n[20];
    char   c[20];
    int    i;

    for (i = 0; i < 20; i = i + 1)
        {
        n[i] = 0;
        c[i] = ' ';
        }
}
```

Notice that i starts the iteration with value zero and finishes at 19. If it were incremented to 20, a memory location outside the bounds of the array would be accessed.

No array-bound checking is done by the C compiler. Beware!

A *string* is a character array terminated by the null character '\0', also known as 'binary zero'.

The standard libraries contain many functions which perform operations on strings. Here are three, which are needed for the program examples:

```
gets (<string>);

atoi (<string>); /* Convert ASCII to
                     integer */

atof (<string>); /* Convert ASCII to
                     float */
```

Using the following definitions:

```
char     instring[20];
int      binval;
double   floatval;
```

then

```
gets     (instring);
```

reads from the standard input device a string of maximum length 20 characters, including the null terminator '\0'. There is nothing to stop the entry of data greater than 20 characters long; if there are more than 20 characters, truncation will ensue.

The terminated character array `instring` may then be converted into its integer numeric equivalent value using the library function 'atoi' as follows:

```
binval = atoi(instring);
```

`instring` may be converted into its double floating-point numeric equivalent value using the library function 'atof':

```
floatval = atof(instring);
```

## 1.11 Pointers

More than any other construct, *pointers* set C apart from all other languages. PL/1 and Pascal have pointers in their syntax, but these are not as flexible in use as C pointers. Use of pointers in C code is ubiquitous.

A variable definition allocates space for the data and associates a name with that data. The data name refers directly to the data stored at the memory location.

Pointers, on the other hand, are data objects which point to other data objects. A pointer is the address of the object pointed to.

A character variable is defined as follows:

```
char c;
```

A character pointer is defined like this:

```
char *cptr;
```

`cptr` is a *pointer to a data object of type 'char'*.

The following statement:

```
cptr = &c;
```

assigns the *address of* c to the *character pointer* `cptr`.

Before this assignment, `cptr` pointed nowhere in particular; after it, `cptr` pointed to the memory location associated with the data name c. Now:

- `cptr` *points to* c.

- `*cptr` is the *'contents of'* or the *'object at'* the pointer `cptr`.

- `*cptr` equals c.

To use a pointer such as `cptr` before the initialising assignment is an error.

Let us make a character pointer point to the array:

```
char instring[20];
```

First, we define a character pointer:

```
char *cptr;
```

Now, we want to assign the address of the array to the character pointer. The address of a simple data item, such as c above, is found using the address operator '&'.

In the case of an array, the address of the array *is the name of the array itself. No '&' operator is needed.*

This is an inconsistency in the C language and causes some trouble.

```
cptr = instring;
```

assigns the address of the array `instring` to the pointer `cptr`.

- `cptr` now points to the first element of the array.

- `*cptr` is the contents of the first element of the array and is the same in meaning as `instring[0]`.

Chapters 6, 7 and 8 describe how pointers may be used to replace the use of subscripts on arrays. Great performance benefits result from this.

Data objects of all types – including pointers themselves – may have pointers. In this introduction, we have only seen character pointers.

## 1.12  C preprocessor

Before a C program is compiled, the source code is processed by the C preprocessor.

The preprocessor deals only with lines of code which have a '#' character as the first non-whitespace character in a line of source code.

The '#' must be followed by a preprocessor keyword. The full set of preprocessor keywords includes the following:

| | |
|---|---|
| define | if |
| include | ifndef |
| ifdef | endif |

For the moment, we will consider only the first two.

We may define symbolic constants with '#define' as follows:

```
#define    PI    3.1415927
#define    MAX    20
```

Wherever MAX is subsequently used in the body of the program source code, the preprocessor, before compilation, converts it into the associated value – in this case, 20.

Note that preprocessor definitions are not terminated with semicolons.

Defining symbolic constants using the preprocessor gives a number of benefits. It helps eliminate 'magic numbers' from the program source. MAX makes more sense, especially to a new reader, than 20.

Secondly, if it is decided to change the value of MAX, it is changed once, where it is defined, rather than at every occurrence throughout the program.

By convention, symbolic constants are written in upper-case, C variables in lower-case.

```
#include "stdio.h"
```

causes inclusion into the program by the preprocessor of the full text of the standard input/output header file 'stdio.h'.

There are other standard header files, such as 'math.h' and 'string.h', which may be similarly included.

The programmer may also write and include original files. Very often, tailor-written include files contain data declarations which it is better not to include explicitly in the program source code.

## Find the error

In each of the programs below, identify the line contaiting the error. Answers are given in Appendix C.

```
1    1   #include "stdio.h"
     2
     3   main ()
     4
     5   {
     6   int n = 5;
     7   char arr[10];
     8
     9   gets (arr);
     10
     11  printf ("Number is %d, string is
                                  %s\n,n, arr);
     12  }


2    1   #include "stdio.h"
     2
     3   main ()
     4
     5   {
     6   int n = 5;
     7   char arr[10];
     8
     9   /* Read in string from standard
            input    * /
     10
     11  gets (arr);
     12
```

```
   13 printf ("Number is %d, string is
                            %s\n",n, arr);
   14 }
```

```
3  1  #include "stdio.h"
   2
   3  main()
   4
   5  {
   6  int n;
   7  char arr[10];
   8
   9  /* Fill array with blanks */
   10
   11 for (n = 0; n < 10; n = n + 1)
   12    arr[n] = ' '
   13 }
```

```
4  1  #include "stdio.h"
   2
   3  main()
   4
   5  {
   6  int n = 5;
   7  int m = 6;
   8  char arr[10];
   9
   10 gets (arr);
   11
   12 printf ("Numbers are %d %d, string
                        is %c\n",n, m, arr);
   13 }
```

```
5  1  int i = 1;
   2  int nums[100];
   3
   4  /* fill array with zeros*/
   5
   6  while (i <= 100)
   7     {
   8     nums[i] = 0;
   9     i = i + 1;
   10    }
```

```
6    1   #include "stdio.h";
     2
     3   main()
     4
     5   {
     6   int n;
     7   char arr[10];
     8
     9   /* Fill array with blanks */
     10
     11  for (n = 0; n < 10; n = n + 1)
     12      arr[n] = ' ';
     13  }
```

```
7    1   #include "stdio.h"
     2
     3   main()
     4
     5   {
     6   int n = 5;
     7   char arr[10];
     8
     9   gets (arr);
     10
     11  printf ("Number is %d, "string" is
                                %s\n",n, arr);
     12  }
```

```
8    1   int a, b, max;
     2
     3   /* initialise  a  and  b  here*/
     4
     5   if a < b
     6       max = b;
     7   else
     8       max = a;
```

```
9    1   char      *cptr;    /* character
                                   pointer*/
     2   char      arr[100];
     3
     4   cptr = &arr;        /* set pointer to
                                array address */
```

# 2 Data Representation in C

![section divider]

## 2.1 Data types

There are four simple data types in C, which are used as type specifiers in the definition of variables:

**char**      a single byte, storing one character

**int**          an integer of a size dependent on the host computer

**float**     a single-precision floating-point (real) number

**double**   a double-precision floating-point (real) number

The simple data types may be qualified with the following keywords:

| | |
|---|---|
| signed | long |
| unsigned | const |
| short | volatile |

C syntax also includes the type specifier 'void', which is explained in Chapters 3 and 8 in terms of function return values, parameters and pointers.

On computers for which the 8-bit byte is the smallest addressable memory space, and therefore the basic data object, the 'char' type specifies a data object of one byte. 'char' is big enough to store any member of the local system's character set.

Even on such computers, the sizes of 'int', 'float' and 'double' data objects vary widely between manufacturers. For reasons of portability, C programmers should take care not to make software dependent on the actual sizes of the data objects; where possible no assumptions should be made about these sizes.

- An 'int' is usually 32 bits (4 bytes) but on some systems is 16 bits.

● A 'float' is usually 32 bits, while a 'double' is usually 64 bits.

The table below gives possibilities for combination of the basic data types and the qualifiers.

|          | char | int | float | double |
|----------|------|-----|-------|--------|
| signed   | X    | X   |       |        |
| unsigned | X    | X   |       |        |
| short    |      | X   |       |        |
| long     |      | X   |       | X      |
| const    | X    | X   | X     | X      |
| volatile | X    | X   | X     | X      |

Whether a data object of type simply 'char' is held as a signed or unsigned value is system-dependent.

'signed char' and 'unsigned char' both occupy the same amount of space. 'unsigned char' means that the data object may not be a negative value. 'signed char' is used to ensure that a 'char' variable can have a negative value; it is not often used, as all members of any character set have positive numeric values.

'signed int' is the default for the 'int' type; the 'signed' qualifier is therefore redundant.

'unsigned int' forces the integer value stored in the data object to be positive. The sign-bit is not used and it is possible to accommodate in an 'unsigned int' a positive value twice as large as for an ordinary 'int'.

If the size of an 'int' is 16 bits, 'short int' is generally also 16 bits while 'long int' is 32 bits. If the 'int' size is 32 bits, 'short int' is generally 16 bits and 'long int' is also 32 bits.

By default, a declaration using the type specifier 'short int' may be simplified to just 'short'. In the same way, 'unsigned' means 'unsigned int' and 'long' means 'long int'.

Depending on the computer, 'long double' may be the same as or longer than 'double'.

The qualifier 'const' may be prefixed to any declaration, and specifies that the value initially assigned to the data object will not be changed.

The qualifier 'volatile' allows the data object which it qualifies to be changed in ways not explicitly specified by the program of which it is part.

For ordinary variable definitions, many C compilers are allowed to carry out optimisation on the assumption that the content of a variable does not change if it does not occur on the left-hand side of an assignment statement. The 'volatile' qualifier causes the suppression of any such optimisation.

'volatile' is put in front of the definition of a variable, as in:

```
volatile int clock;
```

The value of clock might be changed by the local operating system without any assignment to clock in the program. If it were not qualified 'volatile', the value of clock might be corrupted by compiler optimisation.

In addition to the possibilities in the table above, 'signed short int' and 'unsigned short int' are both legal, as are 'signed long int' and 'unsigned long int'.

Here are some example declarations which assume a system with a natural 32-bit integer:

```
short       x;    /* x is 16 bits long and
                     can hold integer values
                     in the range -32767 and
                     32767   */

int         y;    /* y is 32 bits long and
                     holds integer values in
                     the range -2147483647
                     to 2147483647 */

long        z;    /* same as 'int' above */

unsigned short a; /* sign-bit disabled,
                     can hold positive
                     integer values up
                     to 65535 */
```

```
unsigned b;      /* 'int' definition with
                    sign-bit disabled, can
                    hold positive integer
                    values up to 4294967295 */

float    c;      /* c is 32 bits long and
                    can hold a fractional
                    number in a floating-
                    point form in the range
                    10**38 to 10**-38 */

double   d;      /* d is 64 bits long and
                    can hold a fractional
                    number in the range
                    10**308 to 10**-308 */

long double ld;  /* ld is 80 bits long
                    and can hold a fractional
                    number in the range
                    10**4932 to 10**-4932 */
```

Here is a program which finds the largest possible
numeric value which can be stored in an 'int' on the
host computer system:

```
#include "stdio.h"

main()
{
    int shift;
    int accum;

    shift = 1;
    accum = 0;

    /* loop until a further shift would
       set the sign bit */

    while (shift > 0)
        {
        /* add shift to the accumulator and
           double it    */
        accum = accum + shift;
        shift = shift * 2;
        }
    printf ("Maximum int value is %d\n",
            accum);
}
```

This is a rather clever way of solving the problem. The obvious but crude way is to start at 1 and keep adding 1 until the sign-bit changes and the integer goes negative. But on a 32-bit system, this takes somewhat more than two billion additions which, assuming one million per second, will take more than half an hour.

Try running the program to find out the maximum integer size on your system.

The example given does a 'shift and multiply' 32 times and finds the answer according to a logarithmic sequence – literally millions of times faster than by repeated addition.

## 2.2  Variables and identifiers

Variables are defined or declared by association of a type specifier and variable name, as we have already seen. There is a significant difference between declaration and definition, the full rules of which are given in Chapter 3. For simple data objects, declarations and definitions are usually the same; it is enough for now to say that all definitions are declarations but that the converse is not true.

There are in C some simple rules concerning the names that may be used for variables. These names are also called *identifiers*.

A variable name must not be one of the set of C keywords (reserved words). These are:

| | | | |
|---|---|---|---|
| auto | double | int | struct |
| break | else | long | switch |
| case | enum | register | typedef |
| char | extern | return | union |
| const | float | short | unsigned |
| continue | for | signed | void |
| default | goto | sizeof | volatile |
| do | if | static | while |

There are a number of library function names which should not be used as variable names.

A variable name is a sequence of letters and digits. Distinction is made between upper and lower case letters. The underscore character '_' also counts as a character and should be used for clarity in variable names. Punctuation, control and other special characters should not be used in variable names.

While the underscore '_' character may be used as the first character of a variable name, it is unwise to do so. Depending on the operating system in use, certain system routines may exist, the names of which start with the underscore. To avoid a possible clash, the underscore should always be embedded in the variable name in the following way:

```
int     day_of_week;
```

The first character of the variable name must be a letter.

Variable names may be any length, but the C compiler will treat only the first 31 characters as significant – it ignores further characters.

For names of external variables, as described in Chapter 3, only the first six characters are guaranteed to be significant.

Here are some examples of incorrect variable name definitions:

```
int     bank-bal    /* Wrong! incorrect
                        hyphen      */
int     1sttime     /* Wrong! leading
                        number      */
int     new?acc     /* Wrong! invalid
                        character   */
```

## 2.3   Initialisation

It cannot be generally assumed that any variable definition in C will cause that variable to be initialised with a meaningful value. It should be assumed that the contents of an uninitialised variable are garbage.

It is a good thing to explicitly initialise variables at the time they are defined, where it is reasonable to do so.

Consider the variable definitions and initialisations in the maximum-integer example program:

```
int shift;
int accum;

shift = 1;
accum = 0;
```

Instead, the variables can be initialised as part of their definition:

```
int shift = 1;
int accum = 0;
```

A variable of type 'long int' is initialised like this:

```
long big_num = 1000000L;
```

The trailing L explicitly tells the compiler that the 1000000 is to be a long integer.

A variable of type 'char' can be initialised to a character (or numeric) value:

```
char c = 'a';
char d = 97;    /* same thing: 97 is ASCII
                    'a' */
```

Chapters 6 and 7 give the rules for initialisation of more complex data objects and storage classes.

## 2.4 Constants

Constants are such things as the integer 14, the character 'a' and the newline '\n'.

Given the following definitions:

```
int   n;
char  c;
```

it is legal to make these assignments:

```
n = 14;
c = 'a';
```

```
c = '\n';
```

Integer constants are defined as follows:

- The integer constant 14 is a data object of type 'int'.

- 14L or 14l is a long integer – type 'long'.

- 14U or 14u is an unsigned integer constant.

- 14UL is an unsigned long integer constant.

An integer constant too big to be accommodated by an 'int' is taken as a 'long int'.

An integer constant can be prefixed with a leading zero; for example:

```
014
```

This is interpreted as being of base 8 (octal). Octal 014 equals decimal 12.

An integer constant can have the prefix 0x or 0X like this:

```
0x14 or 0X14
0x2F or 0X2F
```

This is interpreted as being of base 16 (hexadecimal). Hexadecimal 0x14 equals decimal 20. 0x2F equals decimal 47.

### Character constants

A character constant is a single character, written between single quotes, like this:

```
'a'
```

A character constant *is a number*. Given the definition and initialisation:

```
char ch = 'a';
```

ch thereafter contains *the numeric value, decimal 97*. Decimal 97 is the numeric representation of 'a' in the ASCII character set, which is used in many micro- and mini-computers. If a different character set is used, for example EBCDIC, the underlying numeric value of 'a' is different. Care should be taken not to write code which involves arithmetic on character constants, where this is dependent on a particular character set. Such code is not generally portable between different systems. Here is an example:

```c
char ch;

/* Initialise  ch  here */

if ((ch >= 'a') && (ch <= 'z'))
    printf ("char %c in range a-z\n",ch);
```

Because the characters 'a' through 'z' are numerically contiguous in the ASCII character set, but not so in, for example, EBCDIC, this code will work as intended only on systems using ASCII.

'0' ('character zero') is a character constant with ASCII value 48. '0' has nothing at all in common with numeric zero, so after the definitions:

```c
int  n = 0;
char c = '0';
```

the integer n contains the value zero; the character c contains the value 48.

### String constants

A string constant looks like this:

```c
"This is a string constant"
```

An array terminated with the null character '\0' is a string.

While a character constant has only one character and is not null-terminated, a string constant (also known as a *string literal*) consists of zero or more characters surrounded by double quotes and is null-terminated. For example:

```c
"This is a string constant"
```

is an array of objects of type 'char' but, in addition, is a null-terminated string. The null character exists only in the internal representation of the string and therefore does not appear in source code.

The null character appended at the end of the array of characters serves as an end-marker for the string. This allows string-processing functions, including many library functions, to know when they have encountered the end of a string.

The double quotes are not part of the string literal; they only delimit the string.

### Floating-point constants

Floating-point constants are always shown as fractional and can be represented in either normal or 'scientific' notation thus:

```
1.0
335.7692
-.00009
31.415927e-1
```

Floating point constants are of type 'double' unless explicitly suffixed with 'f' or 'F', as in:

```
1.7320508F
```

This is of type 'float'.

A floating-point constant suffixed with 'l' or 'L' is of type 'long double'.

### Special character constants

As noted above, the newline character '\n' is a character constant. There is a range of these special character constants – also known as *escape sequences*. They are:

| | |
|---|---|
| \n | newline |
| \r | carriage-return |
| \t | tab |
| \f | formfeed |
| \b | backspace |
| \v | vertical tab |
| \a | audible alarm - BEL |
| \\ | 'escape' backslash |
| \? | 'escape' question-mark |
| \' | 'escape' single quote |
| \" | 'escape' double quote. |

Any or all of these might be used, for example, in a 'printf' statement like this:

```
printf ("This is a double quote
                        symbol: \"\n");
```

This statement prints out:

```
This is a double quote symbol: "
```

It then advances to a new line, as a result of the inclusion of '\n'.

There are many other special characters which do not have an identifying letter and are represented by their number in the character set, delimited by single quotes. These are examples from the ASCII character set:

```
#define  SYN    '\026'   /* ASCII
                           synchronize */
#define  ESC    '\033'   /* ASCII
                           escape      */
```

This is a good use of the preprocessor, equating symbolic constants with numeric control characters. The symbolic constant ESC in the middle of a communications program makes more sense than '\033'.

### Enumeration constant

The enumeration constant is a list of integer constant values; for example:

```
enum seasons {SPRING,SUMMER,AUTUMN,
              WINTER};
```

The four names in this example have values associated with them of 0, 1, 2 and 3 respectively, unless the programmer chooses to depart from the default, like this:

```
enum seasons {SPRING=1,SUMMER=2,
              AUTUMN=3,WINTER=4};
```

Having made either of the above declarations, it is possible to define a variable associated with the enumeration constant:

```
enum seasons time_of_year;
```

`time_of_year` can only have the values SPRING, SUMMER, AUTUMN or WINTER. It is now possible to do a test like this:

```
if (time_of_year == SUMMER)
    go_sunbathing();
```

Arithmetic operations on enumeration constants are illegal.

### Constant expressions

A constant expression is an expression which must evaluate to a constant at compile time. Constant expressions may be used in any context where a constant is legal.

Constant expressions are used in the preprocessor; for array-bound specification; for the values in enumerated data types; in 'switch' statements (Section 5.6); in bit fields (Section 7.6); and in initialiser lists (Chapters 6 and 7).

A constant expression must not contain function calls, assignments, increment, decrement or comma operators (Chapter 4) except when used with the 'sizeof' operator (Section 7.8).

At the end of Chapter 5, there is an example program called 'dates.c', which illustrates most basic C constructs. It uses a tailor-written header file, called 'dates.h', which contains the following definitions and constant expressions:

```
#define    MINYY     0
#define    MAXYY     99
#define    MINMM     1
#define    MAXMM     12
#define    MINDD     1
#define    MAXDD     31
#define    MINFEB    28
#define    MAXFEB    29
#define    TRUE      1
#define    FALSE     0

int idd,imm,iyy;
int mdd[13] = {0,31,28,31,30,31,30,31,
                 31,30,31,30,31};
```

The last definition is of an integer array (mdd) and its initialisation with values which are a zero followed by the numbers of days in each of the months of a year.

The definition could be written slightly differently, but still using only constant expressions in the initialiser list:

```c
int mdd[13] = {0,31,MINFEB,31,MAXDD-1,
               31,MAXDD-1,31,31,MAXDD-1,
               31,MAXDD-1,31};
```

## Find the error

In each of the programs below, identify the line contaning the error. Answers are given in Appendix C.

```
1   1   #include "stdio.h"
    2
    3   main()
    4
    5   {
    6   int    gross_pay, tax-all;
    7   const float tax_rate;
    8   float net_pay;
    9
   10   /* initialise variables with data
           here */
   11
   12   net_pay = gross_pay - ((gross_pay -
                   tax-all) * tax_rate);
   13
   14   printf ("Net pay is %f,\n",net_pay);
   15   }


2   1   #include "stdio.h"
    2
    3   main()
    4
    5   {
    6   int    gross_pay, tax_all;
```

```
 7  float tax_rate;
 8  const float net_pay;
 9
10  /* initialise variables with data
        here */
11
12  net_pay = gross_pay - ((gross_pay -
                 tax_all) * tax_rate);
13
14  printf ("Net pay is %f,\n",net_pay);
15  }
```

**3**
```
 1  /* Compute Einstein's formula*/
 2
 3  unsigned float mass;
 4  long          c;
 5  double        e;
 6
 7  e = mass * (c * c);
```

**4**
```
 1  int   c, switch = 0;
 2
 3  do
 4     {
 5     if (switch == 0)
 6        switch = 1;
 7     else
 8        {
 9        c = getchar();
10        putchar (c);
11        }
12     }
13  while (c != EOF);
```

**5**
```
 1  int   c, sw = 0;
 2
 3  while (c != EOF)
 4     {
 5     if (sw == 0)
 6        sw = 1;
 7     else
 8        {
 9        c = getchar();
```

```
10          putchar (c);
11            }
12      }
```

**6**

```
1   enum seasons (SPRING,SUMMER,
                      AUTUMN,WINTER);
2
3   enum seasons season;
4
5   int dd,mm;
6
7   /* initialise  dd  and  mm  here */
8
9   if ((dd==1) && (mm==2 || mm==5 ||
        mm==8 || mm==11))
10      {
11      /* new season */
12      SPRING = SPRING + 1;
13      }
```

# 3 Functions

## 3.1 Compound statements

A compound statement is a collection of declarations and statements enclosed in a pair of curly braces '{}'.

A compound statement has the general form:

```
{
    <declarations>

    <statements>
}
```

There may be an arbitrary number of declarations and statements. All the declarations must precede the statements.

Compound statements may be nested within compound statements to an arbitrary depth.

The minimal compound statement is:

```
{
}
```

This has no declarations or statements at all.

The 'body' of a function is always a compound statement. Functions are of the general form:

```
<return type><function name>(<parameter
declarations>)

<compound statement>
```

This looks complex, but only the function name, followed by parentheses '()' and a compound statement, are always necessary.

A simple case of a function was given in Chapter 1:

```
myfunc ()
{
    printf ("Hello World again\n");
}
```

'myfunc' is the function name; there are no parameter declarations because no arguments are being passed to the function. The compound statement delimited by the curly braces contains just one 'printf' statement.

## 3.2 Function headers

A function header consists of a return type, the function name and the parameter declarations enclosed in parentheses.

Consider the following definitions and function call:

```
int result, num, n;

result = power(num, n);
```

The header of the called function looks like this:

```
int power(int num, int n)
```

The first 'int' is the function's *return type*. In C, functions, like data objects, have types and this function is of return type 'int'. This means that a value returned by the function to result is of type 'int'.

'int' is the default return type for functions. Only where a function returns an object of type other than 'int' – for example, 'double' or 'char' – must the function return type be specified.

'power', the function name, is an identifier.

In the function call, the *arguments* num and n were supplied as *parameters* to the called function 'power'.

The arguments are sometimes called *actual parameters*, while the parameters are often called *formal parameters*.

The function starts at the first character to the right of the opening parenthesis in the header, which is the first character of the formal parameters.

The formal parameters may be used inside the function in the same way as ordinary variables defined inside the function's main compound statement.

The values of the actual parameters in the call to the function are copied into the formal parameters of the called function. When control is returned from the called function to the statement after the function call, the values of the formal parameters are not returned.

The function header is not a statement and must not be terminated with a semi-colon.

A function header may not occur inside a compound statement; in C, functions may not be nested within functions.

### The ANSI standard

The function header is one of the areas where most changes were made by the ANSI standardisation committee. The 'power' function header above would previously have been written:

```
int power (num, n)
int num, n;
```

This is still legal, but for reasons of improved error- and type-checking by the compiler, it is better to use the ANSI version.

However, many pre-ANSI standard C compilers still exist and are in use. The pre-ANSI form given above, with the definitions of the formal parameters separate from the parameter declarations within parentheses, works with all compilers and may be used in a pre-ANSI environment without affecting portability.

Check on your system whether the compiler in use implements the ANSI standard. You can then write function headers accordingly.

## 3.3 Function return values

As we have seen, a function can return a value to the function which called it.

A function has two ways of returning information to the calling function: by return value and by parameters.

The 'return' statement is used to return a value from a function to where the function was called.

The general form of the 'return' statement is:

```
return <expression>;
```

where the expression is optional.

Use of

```
return;
```

in a function will cause unconditional return of control from the called function to the calling function. No particular value will be returned from the function in this case.

It is more usual to use 'return' in a function to return control to the calling function with a value which is some use in the calling function. Typical uses are these:

```
return (FALSE);
return (ERR_NO);
return (result);
```

The parentheses surrounding the returned expression values are optional.

**Function types**

A function must be of a type: the type of the value it will return. If the function return value is of type 'int', the function type does not have to be explicitly specified because 'int' is the default.

The type of the expression returned is converted, if necessary, to the type of the function containing the 'return'.

Consider the case of the library function 'atof', which converts a string to a double floating-point number like this:

```
#include "stdio.h"

double atof (const char *);
```

```
main ()

{
double    floatval;
char      instring[10];
    .
    /* accept number from standard input */
gets (instring);
    .
    .
    /* convert number from ASCII to float */
floatval = atof (instring);
    .
    /* do something with the number      */
}
```

'atof' is a function of type 'double'; its return value is a floating-point number. Somewhere in 'atof' is a 'return' statement with a 'double' expression.

The function header for 'atof' in the C library looks like this:

```
double atof (const char *str)
```

'atof' is here defined as of type 'double'. This is consistent with the assignment in the program above of the result of 'atof' to a 'double' variable.

Where the return type of a function is not 'int', the function must be *declared* before the first call to it in the body of the program. The line:

```
double atof (const char *);
```

does this and warns the compiler that, somewhere in the body of the program, there is a call to a function called 'atof', which is *defined* as a function of type 'double'.

If 'atof' is not declared in advance in this way, the compiler will expect it to return an 'int' and will treat the return value as such. The result will make no sense.

The 'atof' declaration is in the standard header file 'stdlib.h'. Declaration of 'atof' may, therefore, also be accomplished by inclusion of the 'stdlib.h' header file at the start of the program.

Most functions are of type 'int' by default. They do not have to be declared in advance. When the compiler encounters the function call, it assumes that the function is of return type 'int'.

## Function prototypes

While it is not necessary to declare in advance a function of return type 'int', the ANSI standard specifies that functions of all return types should be declared. The declaration is known as a *function prototype*. Use of function prototypes makes it easier for the compiler to catch errors in the function header and in calls to the function.

In the prototype declaration for 'atof' above, the parameter type is also specified: as a 'char *', or character pointer. In the case of 'atof', this signifies the address of a character array, and could equivalently be written 'char []'. If the parameter type is not specified in the prototype, no checking of parameters between the function call and the function header is done by the compiler.

If the type specifier 'void' is used alone in the prototype parameter declaration list, it indicates that the called function takes no parameters at all. In this case, calling the function with arguments will cause a compiler error.

Variable names may optionally be added to function prototypes.

The following points should be noted:

● This is the first case we have seen of the difference between a declaration and a definition. The function 'atof' is *defined* in its library; it is *declared* in the program to warn the compiler of its presence.

● The return value of many functions is not required by the programmer at all. However, unless specified otherwise, every function has a return value of some kind.

● The type specifier 'void', used as a function's return type, is used to explicitly specify that the function returns no value.

## 3.4 Parameters to functions

The alternative to 'return' for sending back information from a called function is use of *parameters*.

All parameters passed between functions in C are passed *by value*. A call to a function passing parameters by value is known as a *call by value*. Call by value is the only method of parameter passing used by C.

C can also simulate passing parameters *by reference* using the address of (pointer to) the parameter data. A call to a function passing parameters by reference is referred to as a *call by reference*.

The distinction between the two types of call is very important. Call by value means that the values of the actual parameters 'sent' by the calling function are *copied* to the formal parameters that are 'received' by the called function.

Call by reference means that the called function is using *the same data* as that sent by the calling function.

Therefore, call by value does not change the values of the actual parameters in the calling function, no matter what is done to the formal parameters in the called function. Call by reference does change the values of the actual parameters in the calling function.

C is different from other languages in its method of parameter passing. FORTRAN uses call by reference exclusively so that calling and called functions refer to the same parameter data. Pascal has both call by value and call by reference, with the latter being explicitly indicated by means of the 'var' keyword.

Call by reference uses pointers, so this is dealt with fully in Chapter 8. This chapter concentrates on passing parameters between functions by value.

Here is a simple example of passing parameters by value:

```
#include "stdio.h"
float add_nos (int, float); /* prototype */
main ()
{
    int x;
    float y, sum;
    /* initialise  x  and  y  here */
    printf ("Numbers in: %d %f\n", x, y);
    sum = add_nos(x, y);
    printf ("Numbers out: %d %f %f\n",
            x, y, sum);
}
float add_nos (int a, float b)
{
    return (a + b);
}
```

This is an example of overkill: calling a function to add two numbers. However, it makes some good illustrations.

First, the called function 'add_nos' returns its data, converted to type 'float', to the floating-point variable sum in 'main'. This uses 'return', as explained in the last section.

'add_nos' is supplied with its data by means of the actual parameters x and y specified in the function call in 'main'. These values are copied to the formal parameters a and b in the header of 'add_nos'.

In 'main', x is defined as an integer, y as a floating-point value. Their values are copied to a and b in 'add_nos' which are (and must be) defined identically.

It does not matter that the names of the formal parameters are different from those of the actual parameters. They may be the same or different at the discretion of the programmer.

It is vital that the types of the corresponding formal and actual parameters are the same. The formal and actual parameters correspond by position and it is also essential that the order of the actual parameters is the same as that of the formal parameters.

Errors in this area can lead to immediate, nasty and hard-to-find bugs. Pre-ANSI standard C compilers do not help very much. The new function header and function prototype constructs specified in the ANSI standard give considerable improvement in parameter-type checking.

Although, using call by value, the called function cannot change a variable in the calling function, this has a benefit in reducing the scope for error and helping confine bugs within functions.

Call by value is generally useful for simple data types: 'int', 'float' and so on. For aggregate data types there are sometimes some restrictions, which are described in Chapter 7.

**Arrays**

Arrays may be used as parameters passed by value but, in fact, only the address of the array is passed to the called function. As seen in Chapter 1, the name of an array is its address. No copying of array elements between actual and formal parameters takes place. Only the array address is copied. The value of an array passed as a parameter is changed by the called function.

Here is an example that appears in the program 'dates.c':

```c
    int get_data (char [], char [],
                  char []);

    main ()

    {
        char sdd[5],smm[5],syy[5];
        .
        .
        get_data (sdd,smm,syy);
        .
        .
    }

    int get_data (char sdd[],char smm[],
```

```
                    char syy[])
{
    /* get_data function body */
}
```

The addresses of the three character arrays are
passed to the function header 'get_data'. The three
arrays may then be used within 'get_data' in the ordinary way. If the values of the array elements are
changed, the change will affect the values of the arrays in 'main'.

## 3.5    Storage class

Every elementary and aggregate variable has a
*storage class*. The storage class determines the
scope and extent of the variable. Full rules of scope
and extent are explained in the next section; essen-
tially, the storage class of a variable decides within
how much of the program it is 'visible' and how
long it remains in being.

There are two storage classes:

    automatic
    static

Automatic storage is allocated, and de-allocated,
during program execution. Static storage is allocated by the compiler at compile time.

Unless explicitly specified otherwise, a variable
defined within a function (an internal variable) is of
automatic storage class and only exists for the
duration of execution of that function.

A variable defined outside all functions (an external, or global variable) is of static storage class and
exists for the duration of execution of the program.

There are four storage class specifiers which may
be used to specify explicitly a variable's storage
class:

    auto          extern
    static        register

## Automatic storage class

For a variable to be of automatic storage class, it must be defined within a function. All the variables we have so far defined within functions are automatic, or 'auto', data objects.

This means that memory space for these variables is allocated each time the function is entered and that the space is discarded upon exit from the function. Because of this, an automatic variable cannot be accessed from any other function. The value of an automatic variable is lost on exit from the function in which it is defined.

An integer definition can be as follows:

```
int x;
```

If this is within a function and not otherwise qualified, it means the same thing as:

```
auto int x;
```

However, 'auto' is the default storage class specifier and need not be explicitly declared. (It rarely is.)

## The 'register' specifier

A variable may be defined with the storage class specifier 'register'. 'register' is the same as 'auto' in all ways except that the compiler, on seeing the 'register' specifier, attempts to allocate space for the variable in a high-speed machine register, if such is available.

There is only a limited number of machine registers, so the 'register' storage class specifier should be used sparingly. It is best used in the case of a small, heavily used variable such as an array subscript or loop counter.

'register' variables cannot be accessed with pointers. There is no guarantee that a machine register will be allocated as a result of the 'register' specification. Usually, a moderate performance improvement is to be expected if 'register' is used well.

The following is an example of a 'register' variable definition:

```
register int sub;
```

## Static storage class

A variable is defined with static storage class if it is defined outside all functions or if the keyword 'static' is prefixed to its definition. A static variable has its memory allocated at program compilation time, rather than in the transient way we have seen for 'auto'.

A variable defined within a function may be explicitly specified 'static'. This static internal variable retains its value even on exit from that function. A static internal variable cannot be accessed by other functions in the program, but a value assigned to it will still exist the next time the function is entered.

An external variable is, by default, of static storage class. To explicitly specify an external variable as 'static' – a static external variable – gives it an extra meaning which will be explained in the next section.

If a static variable is not explicitly initialised, its value will be set to zero at compile time, when space for it is allocated. This is an exception referred to in Section 2.3, Initialisation. Definition of a variable with explicit specification of static storage class looks like this:

```
static double floatval;
```

## The 'extern' specifier

The last storage class specifier is 'extern'. An external variable may be accessed by any function in the program file in which it is defined. Its definition may be accessed by any function in another program file if it is *declared* in that program file with the prefix 'extern'.

Here is an example of the use of 'extern' based on the example program 'dates.c'. Some external variables are defined. These may be used throughout the program file 'dates.c'. They may also be referenced from the file 'julian.c', used only for this illustration, which also requires the data.

```
/* Program file 'dates.c'   */

/* External (global) definitions */

int    idd, iyy, imm;
int    mdd[13] =    {0,31,28,31,30,31,30,
                     31,31,30,31,30,31};
int get_data (char [], char [], char []);
int julian (void);

main()

{
   /* External variables visible here */
}

int get_data(char dd[], char mm[],
             char yy[])

{
   /* External variables visible here and
      in all other functions in the
      program file 'dates.c'   */
}

/* Other 'dates.c' functions follow */

/* Program file 'julian.c' */

/* External reference to global
   variables in 'dates.c'   */

extern int idd, imm, iyy;
extern int mdd[13];

int julian(void)

{
   /* Global variables, defined in
      'dates.c' and declared and
      referenced externally in
      'julian.c', may be used here and
      throughout the program file
      julian.c */
}
```

Functions are not variables, but they are external objects: they are accessible throughout the whole program file. Remember: the start of a function is the first character to the right of the opening parenthesis, in front of the formal parameter declarations. All data objects declared within a function are internal. The function name is external because it is not part of the function itself.

## 3.6   Scope and extent

The *scope* of a data object is the region of the program where it is 'visible' and may be used. The *extent* of a data object is the duration of its existence.

The scope of a data object depends on its storage class and on whether it is internal or external.

### Internal variables

All internal variables, whether of static or automatic storage class, have scope limited to the function within which they are defined.

All formal parameters to a function are internal objects and are in scope only within that function.

Bearing in mind that a compound statement is of the form:

```
{
    <declarations>

    <statements>
}
```

all variables declared within a compound statement are internal and have scope limited to that compound statement. Since the body of a function is a compound statement, it is usual to define all variables needed by the function at the start of the compound statement. It is possible to define variables within a subsidiary compound statement, as this example shows:

```
int myfunc (int a, float b)

{
    int x,y;
        .
        .
        .
    if (x == a)
        {
          int c;
          int y;
              .
              .
              .
        }
}
```

a, b, x, y, and c are all internal variables.

● a and b are in scope from the point of their declaration to the end of the function.

● x is in scope from just after the opening curly brace of the function's main compound statement to the end of the function.

● c is in scope from the opening curly brace of the compound statement that is subject to the 'if', to the end of that compound statement.

● y, as defined at the top of the principal function compound statement, is in scope for the whole function, except that it is not in scope for the extent of y, as defined in the compound statement subject to the 'if'. For that period, the first definition and value of y is replaced by the second.

This double use of y is called *masking* and, for the sake of program clarity, is a bad idea. It is also a bad idea to make declarations at a level of compound statement lower than that of the function.

Static internal variables have the same scope as automatic internal variables – the function in which they are defined – but their extent is different. An automatic internal's extent is the duration of execution of the function in which it is declared. A static internal's extent is the whole program file.

### External variables

To explicitly specify an external variable 'static' causes it to be out of scope for the functions of program files other than the one in which it was defined.

Likewise, a function name prefixed with the storage class specifier 'static' will be out of scope for functions in other program files.

Assuming non-use of the 'static' specifier, if an external variable is defined in a program file, it may be referenced by the functions of another program file by means of a declaration of the same data object. The declaration must contain the prefix 'extern'.

If an external variable is defined in a program file, but not at the start, it is not in scope in any functions in the program file which precede its definition. Declaration of the external variable, at the top of the program file outside all functions, brings its definition into scope for all such functions.

The definition of an external variable should only occur once in all the program files, although there may be many declarations of the variable with 'extern'.

Use of 'extern' is another case which illustrates the difference between declaration and definition. The full rules for declaration and definition are given later in this chapter.

### Functions

Functions, as well as variables, have scope. Functions may not be nested: all functions are therefore external objects.

In general, a function definition is not in scope in the part of the program which precedes its definition. In practice, this would make C unworkable – there would be no way of calling a function 'lower' in the source code.

To allow for this, functions, as well as being defined, may be declared. As we have seen, functions returning a data object of type 'int' do not have to be declared in advance. However, to meet the ANSI standard requirements these and all other functions should be declared with a prototype. Recall the earlier use of the library function 'atof', which returns a 'double':

```
#include "stdio.h"
double atof (const char *);

main()

{
double    floatval;
char      instring[10];

    .
    /* accept number from standard
       input */
gets (instring);

    .
    .
    /* convert number from ASCII to
       float */
floatval = atof (instring);

    .
    /* do something with the number */
}
```

The declaration of 'atof' tells the compiler that a function called 'atof' is somewhere defined and that any subsequent call to the function will be in scope.

Here the declaration of 'atof' is in scope throughout the program file. It is also possible to declare a function within a function. If the declaration of 'atof' were within 'main', a call to 'atof' would only be in scope after its declaration in 'main' and up to the end of 'main'.

The compiler assumes, upon seeing a function call without a previous declaration, that the function is defined elsewhere and that it is of type 'int'. An integer function is always in scope and does not have to be declared, although declaration is recommended.

## 3.7 Declaration and definition

The terms declaration and definition are often interchangeable but there is a crucial difference.

A *declaration* specifies a data object with a name, type and storage class, but *it does not allocate any space for the data* in memory.

A *definition* is a declaration which additionally allocates space for the data object.

A definition is a less general case of a declaration. Every definition is an *instantiation* of a declaration.

The places so far where we have seen a difference between declaration and definition are:

- Declaration of a function in advance to warn the compiler of its subsequent definition

- Enumeration constants, for which a declaration is followed by definition of instance(s) of the enumeration list

- In the case of external variables, definition of a global variable in one program file which is declared in other program file(s) by means of the 'extern' storage class specifier

Chapter 7 includes the rules for declaration of aggregate data types and their definition as well as those for constructing, declaring and defining objects of original data types.

## 3.8 Header files

Header files have been described previously; immediately before compilation of the program 'dates.c', the C preprocessor includes (with '#include') the standard header file 'stdio.h' and a custom-made one, 'dates.h'.

Function and macro declarations in the standard header files correspond to function definitions in the standard C libraries. If C library functions are called in a program, the appropriate standard header file(s) should be included in the program (with '#include') to declare the functions.

As programs – and the amount of data, declarations and constants they use – grow bigger during development, it is a good thing to centralise in one programmer-defined header file as many as possible of the declarations that are common to all source files in the program.

A single, standard version of a header file containing many declarations necessary for many different programs stands a better chance of being isolated and, therefore, not being corrupted during change.

Header files may include other header files to an arbitrary depth, but it makes programs hard to read if nesting of header files is more than one or two deep.

A header file is included by the preprocessor in program source code thus:

```
#include "dates.h"
```

The '.h' suffix is only a convention; it denotes 'header' file.

The use of double quotes around the header file name tells the preprocessor to look for the header file in the user's own directory as well as the standard system directories.

It is possible to use angle-brackets < > instead of the double quotes, as in:

```
#include <dates.h>
```

This causes the preprocessor to search only in the standard system directories.

When the preprocessor finds the header file, it substitutes its full text for the '#include' directive in the program source code.

## 3.9 Recursion

It is possible for a function to call itself; this process is known as *recursion*.

Recursion is mainly useful for doing jobs which can be defined in terms of the job itself. Examples include sorting a large set of objects by the method of sorting successively smaller subsets, traversing binary trees and computing factorials.

When a function calls itself recursively, on each recursive call to the function a new set of all automatic variables is allocated. The values of the automatic variables for each successive recursive call to the function are stored in a conceptual 'stack'. When the lowest level of recursion is reached, the recursion 'unwinds' back up the stack of function calls and data.

Care needs to be taken not to get into an infinite recursive calling sequence: this will rapidly exhaust all system memory.

Here is a standard simple example of a recursive program which prints out numbers in ascending order:

```c
#include "stdio.h"

int prlist(int);

main ()
{
    prlist (10);
}

int prlist (int num)
```

```
{
   if (num > 1)
      prlist (num - 1);
   printf ("%d\n", num);
}
```

Trace the program carefully, keeping in mind that every time 'prlist' is called, a new variable num is allocated. 'prlist' calls itself nine times and then ten 'printf' statements 'unwind' and print out the numbers in ascending order.

To write more complex recursive programs, the concept of function 'call by reference' is useful. This is described in Chapter 8.

## Find the error

In each of the programs below, identify the line contaiing the error. Answers are given in Appendix C.

```
1   1  #include "stdio.h"
    2
    3  float do_net_pay (int, int, float);
    4
    5  main ()
    6
    7  {
    8  int    gross_pay, tax_all;
    9  const float tax_rate;
   10  float net_pay;
   11
   12  /* initialise variables with data
          here */
   13
   14  net_pay = do_net_pay (gross_pay,
                   tax_all, tax_rate);
   15
   16  printf ("Net pay is %f,\n", net_pay);
   17  }
   18
   19  float do_net_pay (int gross_pay,
           int tax_all, float tax_rate);
   20  {
```

```
   21 float net_pay;
   22
   23 net_pay = (gross_pay - (gross_pay -
                  tax_all) * tax_rate);
   24 return (net_pay);
   25 }
```

**2**
```
   1  #include "stdio.h"
   2
   3  float do_net_pay (int, int, float);
   4
   5  main()
   6
   7  {
   8  int   gross_pay, tax_all;
   9  const float tax_rate;
   10 float net_pay;
   11
   12 /* initialise variables with data
       here */
   13
   14 net_pay = do_net_pay (gross_pay,
                  tax_all, tax_rate);
   15
   16 printf ("Net pay is %f,\n",net_pay);
   17 }
   18
   19 float do_net_pay (int gross_pay,
           float tax_all, float tax_rate)
   20 {
   21 float net_pay;
   22
   23 net_pay = (gross_pay - (gross_pay -
                  tax_all) * tax_rate);
   24 return (net_pay);
   25 }
```

**3**
```
   1  #include "stdio.h"
   2
   3  do_net_pay (int, int, float);
   4
   5  main()
   6
   7  {
```

```
 8  int   gross_pay, tax_all;
 9  const float tax_rate;
10  float net_pay;
11
12  /* initialise variables with data
       here */
13
14  net_pay = do_net_pay (gross_pay,
                   tax_all, tax_rate);
15
16  printf ("Net pay is %f,\n",net_pay);
17  }
18
19  float do_net_pay (int gross_pay,
            int tax_all, float tax_rate)
20  {
21  float net_pay;
22
23  net_pay = (gross_pay - (gross_pay -
                  tax_all) * tax_rate);
24  return (net_pay);
25  }
```

```
4   1  #include "stdio.h"
    2
    3  float do_net_pay (int, int, float);
    4
    5  main ()
    6
    7  {
    8  int   gross_pay, tax_all;
    9  const float tax_rate;
   10  float net_pay;
   11
   12  /* initialise variables with data
          here */
   13
   14  net_pay = do_net_pay (gross_pay,
                      tax_all, tax_rate);
   15
   16  int pension, emp_age;
   17
   18  /* read in pension and age here*/
   19
```

```
20 if (emp_age > 25)
21    net_pay = net_pay - pension;
22 printf ("Net pay is %f,\n",net_pay);
23 }
24
25 float do_net_pay (int gross_pay,
          int tax_all, float tax_rate)
26 {
27 float net_pay;
28
29 net_pay = (gross_pay - (gross_pay -
              tax_all) * tax_rate);
30 return (net_pay);
31 }
```

```
5  1  #include "stdio.h"
   2
   3  float do_net_pay (int, int, float);
   4
   5  main()
   6
   7  {
   8  int   gross_pay, tax_all;
   9  const float tax_rate;
  10  float net_pay;
  11  int pension, emp_age;
  12
  13  /* initialise variables with data
      here */
  14
  15  net_pay = do_net_pay (gross_pay,
                  tax_all, tax_rate);
  16
  17  /* read in pension and age here*/
  18
  19  if (emp_age > 25)
  20     net_pay = net_pay - pension;
  21  printf ("Net pay is %f,\n",net_pay);
  22  }
  23
  24  do_net_pay (int gross_pay, int
              tax_all, float tax_rate)
  25  {
  26  float net_pay;
```

```
   27
   28 net_pay = (gross_pay - (gross_pay -
                 tax_all) * tax_rate);
   29 return (net_pay);
   30 }
```

```
6   1   #include "stdio.h"
    2
    3   float do_net_pay (int, int, float);
    4
    5   main()
    6
    7   {
    8   int    gross_pay, tax_all;
    9   const float tax_rate;
   10   float net_pay;
   11   int pension, emp_age;
   12
   13   /* initialise variables with data
         here */
   14
   15   net_pay = do_net_pay (gross_pay,
                      tax_all, tax_rate);
   16
   17   /* read in pension and age here*/
   18
   19   if (emp_age > 25)
   20      net_pay = net_pay - pension;
   21   printf ("Net pay is %f,\n",net_pay);
   22
   23   float do_net_pay (int gross_pay,
            int tax_all, float tax_rate)
   24   {
   25   float net_pay;
   26
   27   net_pay = (gross_pay - (gross_pay -
                 tax_all) * tax_rate);
   28   return (net_pay);
   29   }
   30   }
```

```
7   1   #include "stdio.h"
    2
    3   float do_net_pay (int, int, float);
```

```
4
5  main()
6
7  {
8  int    gross_pay, tax_all;
9  const float tax_rate;
10 float net_pay;
11 int pension, emp_age;
12
13 /* initialise variables with data
      here */
14
15 net_pay = do_net_pay (gross_pay,
                  tax_all, tax_rate);
16
17 /* read in pension and age here*/
18
19 if (emp_age > 25)
20    net_pay = net_pay - pension;
21 printf ("Net pay is %f,\n",net_pay);
22 }
23
24 float do_net_pay (int gross_pay,
          int tax_all, float tax_rate)
25 {
26
27 net_pay = (gross_pay - (gross_pay -
               tax_all) * tax_rate);
28 return (net_pay);
29 }
```

```
8  1  #include "stdio.h"
   2
   3  float do_net_pay (int, int, float);
   4
   5  main()
   6
   7  {
   8  int    gross_pay, tax_all;
   9  const float tax_rate;
   10 float net_pay;
   11 int pension, emp_age;
   12
```

```
13 /* initialise variables with data
      here */
14
15 net_pay = do_net_pay (gross_pay,
                  tax_all, tax_rate);
16
17 /* read in pension and age here*/
18
19 if (emp_age > 25)
20     {
21     net_pay = net_pay - pension;
22 printf ("Net pay is %f,\n",net_pay);
23 }
24
25 float do_net_pay (int gross_pay,
          int tax_all, float tax_rate)
26 {
27 float net_pay;
28
29 net_pay = (gross_pay - (gross_pay -
                  tax_all) * tax_rate);
30 return (net_pay);
31 }
```

# 4 Expressions, Operators and Precedence

## 4.1 Boolean value of expressions

Every C expression has an inherent value, which is either zero or non-zero. Zero is 'false'; non-zero is 'true'.

Unlike, for example, Pascal, C has no specific data type 'boolean'. An 'int' or 'short' type may be used where a boolean variable is required:

```
short date_valid = 0;   /* set FALSE   */
        .
        .
        .
/* Assign return-value of
   date-validation function to the flag.
   The return value is either 0 (FALSE)
   or 1 (TRUE).          */

date_valid = validate();

if (date_valid == 1)
    printf ("Valid date entered.\n");
if (date_valid == 0)
    printf ("Invalid date entered.\n");
```

With some preprocessor definitions, it is possible to improve this code, as follows:

```
#define  boolean  short
#define  TRUE     1
#define  FALSE    0
        .
        .
        .
boolean  date_valid = FALSE;
        .
        .
        .
date_valid = validate();
```

```
if (date_valid == TRUE)
    printf ("Valid date entered\n");
if (date_valid == FALSE)
    printf ("Invalid date entered\n");
```

Recall that every expression has a zero or non-zero value. We can simplify the last four lines:

```
if (date_valid)
    printf ("Valid date entered\n");

if (!date_valid)
    printf ("Invalid date entered\n");
```

If date_valid is not zero, it is 'true' and the first test succeeds. If date_valid is zero, it is 'false'. The unary negation operator '!' causes the second test to go true and an invalid date is flagged.

In this example, the function call

```
validate ()
```

is itself an expression with an inherent return value. It is legal to write:

```
if ((validate()) == TRUE)
    /* return value true, date valid*/
    printf ("Valid date entered\n");
```

or simply:

```
if (validate())
    printf ("Valid date entered\n");
```

For expressions, value zero represents 'false'; non-zero is 'true'. For relational expressions, 'false' equals zero and 'true' equals 1.

To illustrate:

```
int      a = 0;
int      b = -5;
int      c = 5;
float    e = 2.71828;

a        /* FALSE    */
b        /* TRUE     */
a + b    /* TRUE     */
b + c    /* FALSE    */
e        /* TRUE     */
```

```
a == 0    /* TRUE (1)    */
b <  0    /* TRUE (1)    */
e > 3.0   /* FALSE (0)   */
```

Finally, the explicit values 1 and 0 may themselves be used to represent 'true' and 'false':

```
while (1)    /* infinite loop */
while (!0)   /* same          */
```

## 4.2  Assignment

So far we have seen only the simple assignment operator '='. It has the effect of changing the value of the operand to its left. This operand is sometimes called the 'lvalue'.

The 'lvalue' operand to the left of the assignment must be an expression referring to a region of memory which the program may change. Therefore, it must not be a constant or an expression like x + 5.

```
short no_leaps;
        .
        .
        .
no_leaps = 0;  /* assignment changes the
                  value stored at the
                  location associated
                  with the name no_leaps
                  to zero       */
```

To add 1 to the value of no_leaps:

```
no_leaps = no_leaps + 1;
```

This means that the memory location named no_leaps is updated with the current value stored in that memory location plus one.

In C, the statement may also be written:

```
no_leaps++;
```

This has the same effect on no_leaps. It is shorter and, depending on the compiler, may lessen compile time and reduce resultant code output, because there is only one reference to the variable being incremented.

To decrement by one:

```
no_leaps = no_leaps - 1;
```

This may be written:

```
no_leaps--;
```

If we wanted to increment no_leaps by 2, we could write:

```
no_leaps = no_leaps + 2;
```

or:

```
no_leaps += 2;
```

In C, for the general assignment:

```
<expr1> = <expr1> <op> <(expr2)>
```

it is possible to substitute:

```
<expr1> <op>= <expr2>
```

where <op>= is a compound assignment operator.

| | | |
|---|---|---|
| x += y | is equivalent to | x = x + y |
| x *= y + z | is equivalent to | x = x * (y + z) |
| x -= y | is equivalent to | x = x - y |
| x /= y | is equivalent to | x = x / y |

Importantly, the expression to the right of the compound assignment operator is always evaluated before the operator. For example:

```
x *= y + z;
```

This does not mean:

```
x = x * y + z;
```

which, by the normal precedence rules, is:

```
x = (x * y) + z;
```

Instead, it means:

```
x = x * (y + z);
```

Compound assignment operators are lower in precedence of evaluation than any other operator except the comma, which is described later in this chapter.

The next section covers the other C binary operators; all of these may also be used in compound assignment operators.

The most common of all compound assignments is the 'increment by one', as in:

```
no_leaps++;
```

It is also legal to use:

```
++no_leaps;
```

If no_leaps is the only operand in the expression and this expression is not itself on the right-hand side of an assignment, the two statements above are equivalent.

In the following case, the uses of the '++' compound operator before and after the variable are not equivalent:

```
int    days_total;
    .
    .
    .
days_total = no_leaps++;
```

Here, the value of no_leaps is assigned to days_total and *only then* is no_leaps incremented by one.

If the statement were instead written:

```
days_total = ++no_leaps;
```

the value of no_leaps would be incremented first and then assigned to days_total.

This and the other rules of precedence are explained in Section 4.8. For now, it is enough to point out the importance of the ordering of operators, operands and parentheses.

## 4.3 Arithmetic and relational operators

The arithmetic operators are:

| | |
|---|---|
| + | addition |
| - | subtraction |
| * | multiplication |
| / | division |
| % | modulus |

Use of the division operator '/' with two or more integer operands causes integer division and consequent truncation:

| | |
|---|---|
| 3/5 | equals zero |
| 5/3 | equals 1 |

The modulus or 'remainder' operator '%' may only be used with operands of basic type 'int' or 'char'. It must not be used with 'float' or 'double'.

Multiplication, division and modulus operations are done before addition and subtraction. Unary minus operations are carried out before any of these.

```
int     x = 5;
int     y = 6;
int     z = 7;
int     result;

  .

  .

  .

result = x + y * z;       /* result == 47*/
result = y / x * z;       /* result == 7 */
result = (x + y) * z;     /* result == 77*/
result = -y * z + x;      /* result == -37*/
result = z / x % y;       /* result == 1 */
```

The relational operators are:

| | |
|---|---|
| < | less than |
| > | greater than |
| <= | less than or equal to |
| >= | greater than or equal to |

The equality operators are:

| == | equality |
| != | non-equality |

All arithmetic operations are done before relational tests, which in turn are carried out before tests for equality. For example:

```
if (idd > MAXDD - 1)
```

means the same as:

```
if (idd > (MAXDD - 1))
```

However, the latter form may often be used for clarity.

As with usage of the arithmetic operators, liberal employment of parentheses can eliminate surprises caused by unexpected effects of the precedence rules.

## 4.4   Logical and bitwise operators

C's logical operators are:

| && | AND |
| \|\| | OR |
| ! | NOT |

The precedence of the unary negation operator '!' is the same as that of unary minus '-' and is higher than any of the arithmetic, relational, logical or bitwise operators.

'&&' and '||' operations are of lower precedence than relational and equality operations. '&&' is evaluated before '||'.

For example:

```
if (imm==4 || imm==6 || imm==9 ||
    imm==11 && idd > 30)
```

In this case, parentheses are not necessary around the individual conditions, although they may be useful for clarity and logical correctness. Each of the equality tests and the greater-than test is of higher precedence than any of the relational operations.

Evaluation will be unexpected in one way: the first test is done for imm being equal to 11 AND idd being more than 30. If the month is one of 4, 6 or 9, the test returns TRUE (1) regardless of the value of idd.

To achieve what was probably required, parentheses should be used:

```
if ((imm==4 || imm==6 || imm==9 ||
    imm==11) && (idd > 30))
```

There is no logical (other than bit-level) exclusive-or operator in C. The exclusive-or – 'either a OR b but not both' – can be achieved with the construct:

```
((a && !b) || (b && !a))
```

It is possible in C to do operations directly at bit level on integer variables. Such operations – often called bit twiddling! – are mainly useful in system and communications programming, and in applications where space is at a premium.

Bit twiddling is further explored in Chapter 10; the bitwise operators, with simple examples of their use, are introduced here.

The bitwise operators are these:

| & | bitwise AND |
|---|---|
| \| | bitwise OR |
| ^ | bitwise exclusive OR |
| ~ | one's complement |
| >> | right bit shift |
| << | left bit shift |

The precedence of these operators is lower than the arithmetic and relational operators, but higher than '&&' and '||'.

Only data objects of type integer may be used as operands for the bitwise operators.

Suppose that the following definitions are made:

```
#define  DEV_TX    0x00000001
#define  DEV_RX    0x00000002
```

```
#define   DEV_WAIT 0x00000004
#define   BUF_FULL 0x00000008

      .
      .
      .

int       state_flag = 0;
```

The bit patterns of the last eight bits of the data objects look like this:

| | | | |
|---|---|---|---|
| DEV_TX | 00000001 | hex | 1 |
| DEV_RX | 00000010 | hex | 2 |
| DEV_WAIT | 00000100 | hex | 4 |
| BUF_FULL | 00001000 | hex | 8 |
| state_flag | 00000000 | zero | |

To set the flag to DEV_TX (transmit), use:

```
state_flag |= DEV_TX;
```

This ORs the rightmost bit of state_flag with the pre-set rightmost bit of DEV_TX and sets state_flag to this bit pattern:

```
00000001
```

When transmit data runs out, we may set the device in a wait state:

```
state_flag |= DEV_WAIT;
```

The state_flag bit pattern now looks like this:

```
00000101
```

Now, suppose we want to check whether the device is receiving or the device buffer is full. We can test the status of DEV_RX and BUF_FULL like this:

```
if (state_flag & DEV_RX)
    printf ("Device in receive mode.\n");
if (state_flag & BUF_FULL)
    printf ("Device receive buffer full.\n");
```

Both of the tests logically AND the bit constants with state_flag. Because, in state_flag, neither the second- nor the fourth-last bits is set to one, both tests will fail.

If, for some reason, it were required to shift the bits in state_flag, this would be done using the shift operators:

```
/* state_flag   00000101 */

/* now left-shift bits by two places*/
state_flag <<= 2;
/* state_flag   00010100 */

/* now right-shift by three places*/
state_flag >>= 3;
/* state_flag   00000010 */
```

## 4.5   The Comma operator

The comma operator is most often used in the 'for' statement. It is also possible to use it elsewhere to guarantee the order of evaluation of sub-expressions.

The comma operator ',' has the lowest precedence of all C operators.

In the 'for' statement the comma might be used like this:

```
for (i = 0, c = getchar(); i < MAX &&
     c != EOF; i++, c = getchar())
    {
    /* do something with  i  and  c*/
    }
```

Sub-expressions separated by comma operators are guaranteed to be evaluated in left-to-right order. The return value of the whole expression (where the sub-expressions are operands of the comma operator) is the value of the rightmost sub-expression.

In the 'for' statement above, the initialising statements set i to zero and get a character, in that order. A compound condition terminates the loop. On each iteration, i is incremented and a character read, in that order.

The order of evaluation can be vital:

```
int    sub;
char   arr[10];

sub = 0, arr[sub] = '\0';
```

If the assignment of the NULL character to the array were done first, its subscript sub would contain a garbage value and would probably cause an array-bound overflow.

The comma operator is not to be confused with the comma when it is used as a separator. The comma as a separator is used as follows:

● In multi-variable declarations:

```
int i, j;
```

● To separate function arguments:

```
printf ("Root of %d is %f \n", n++,
    sqrt(n));
```

● In initialiser lists for arrays and structures

Commas used as separators do not guarantee the order of evaluation of expressions which they may separate. The value of 'sqrt(n)' in the 'printf' statement above is system-dependent, because the C language does not specify whether n is incremented before or after the call to the square-root library function.

As a further illustration of the difference between the comma operator and the comma separator, consider the following function calls:

```
func1 (exp1, exp2);

func2 ((exp1, exp2));
```

'func1' receives two formal parameters, *exp1* and *exp2*, which are separated in the syntax by a comma.

'func2', on the other hand, receives only one formal parameter: the value of *exp2*, which is the return value of the expression containing *exp1*, *exp2* and a comma operator.

## 4.6  Conditional expressions

The conditional operator '?' allows a shorthand to be used for 'if....else' constructs such as:

```
if (x > y)
    max = x;
else
    max = y;
```

Using '?', this may be written:

```
max = (x > y) ? x : y;
```

The parentheses around the condition are not necessary; the '?' is of lower precedence than any of the arithmetic or logical operators.

Whether or not the condition expression is enclosed in parentheses, it is evaluated first; one, and only one, of the second and third operands is evaluated, depending on the boolean result of the condition expression.

The parentheses, even in this simple case, are nevertheless useful for readability.

Use of the '?' operator causes the compiler to generate more efficient code than the 'if....else' equivalent. The price is in code readability.

For a more complex example:

```
if ((imm == 2) && (idd == 29))
    (iyy % 4) > 0 ?
    printf ("Not leap year, Feb 29
                            invalid\n");
    printf ("Leap year, Feb 29 OK\n");
```

Care needs to exercised in use of conditional expressions; otherwise, impenetrable and unreadable code is produced as a result.

## 4.7  Expression evaluation

As we have already seen, the order in which expressions are evaluated is very important.

The rules of C for operator precedence and associativity in the evaluation of expressions are given in full in the next section. These rules define the order in which an expression's operations are evaluated. In general, C does not specify the order in which the operands of an operator are fetched from memory and evaluated. For instance:

```
printf ("Root of %d is %f\n",n++,
        sqrt(n));
```

Here, we cannot be sure whether the root found will be that of n or n + 1, since no certainty exists as to whether n++ or sqrt(n) will be evaluated first. The evaluation is system-dependent.

Similarly:

```
total = x++ - x++;
```

The result of this statement is unpredictable; total may be assigned either of the values -1 or zero, depending on the order in which the two instances of x are fetched.

Except in the case of a few operators, no assumptions should be made by the programmer as to the order in which operands will be evaluated.

The exceptions are the relational operators '&&' and '||', the conditional expression operator '?' and the comma operator.

The comma and conditional operators by definition guarantee the order of evaluation of their operands.

Operands of the logical AND and OR operators are evaluated from left to right until (and only until) the boolean result of the condition is determined. Consider this case:

```
if ((idd < MINDD) || (idd > MAXDD))
    return (FALSE);
```

If the first condition is true, idd is not checked for being greater than the maximum.

Problems can arise with this:

```
if ((x == 5) && ((c = getchar())
    != EOF))
  {
  /* do something    */
  }
/* process   c      */
```

If x is not equal to 5, the character is not read and the processing of c after the 'if' statement will be on the wrong input character.

## 4.8   Operator precedence and associativity

C's rules of precedence and associativity determine the order in which the operations making up the evaluation of an expression will take place.

Precedence is a formalisation of the familiar (and not so familiar) rules of operator evaluation order.

From the conventions of simple arithmetic, we expect:

```
a * b + c
```

to be evaluated as:

```
(a * b) + c
```

and not:

```
a * (b + c)
```

Some conventions hold that division is of higher precedence than multiplication, but in C they are the same, along with the modulus operator %.

Addition and subtraction are of the same precedence relative to each other, but lower than the other arithmetic operators.

Associativity is subordinate to precedence: when two operators are of the same precedence, the order of evaluation of the expression is controlled by their associativity.

The operators' precedence is equal in this case:

```
a / b * c
```

The operators associate left-to-right, so the division takes place before the multiplication.

The full table of operator precedence and associativity is given below. A few operators are included that have not yet been encountered. These are mainly concerned with advanced use of pointers, where precedence of pointer operators becomes important.

| Operators | Associativity |
|---|---|
| () [] -> . | left to right |
| ! ~ ++ -- + - * & (type) sizeof | right to left |
| * / % | left to right |
| + - | left to right |
| << >> | left to right |
| < > <= >= | left to right |
| == != | left to right |
| & | left to right |
| ^ | left to right |
| \| | left to right |
| && | left to right |
| \|\| | left to right |
| ? : | right to left |
| = += -= *= /= %= &= ^= \|= <<= >>= | right to left |
| , | left to right |

Unary '-', '+' and '*' are of higher precedence than the same operators used with binary operands.

The '()' operator means the parentheses in a function call.

The '[]' operator means array-bound square brackets.

'->' and '.' are the 'pointer to' and 'member of' operators for structures, which are described in Chapter 7.

'*' is, as well as multiplication, the pointer 'dereferencer' (object at a pointer).

'&' is the 'address of' a variable.

If you can remember the order of precedence and associativity for all operators in C, fine. Otherwise, *use parentheses*, even if they are not strictly necessary. It costs nothing to use the parentheses. It also saves errors and improves code readability.

## 4.9 Expression type

Every expression has a type: the type of the 'lvalue' if the expression is an assignment or the type of the data object returned by the expression.

The expression type is determined recursively by the types of its constituent sub-expressions. If all the operands in an expression are of a given type, that type is also the type of the expression. For example, consider the definitions:

```
int a, b, c, d;
```

In this case, the expression:

```
a + b * c / d
```

is of type 'int'.

Very often, operators within an expression have operands of different types. Where this is the case, the operand types are automatically converted by the compiler to give the most sensible possible result.

Think of 'char' as being the 'lowest' type and of 'long double' being the 'highest'. If two operands of a sub-expression are of different types, the 'lower' type is forced upwards or 'promoted' to the 'higher' type.

For a sub-expression with two operands and one operator, arithmetic type promotion is governed by the following rules:

- If two operands are of different types, the 'lower' type is converted to the 'higher' type:

  - If one operand is of type 'long double', the other operand is converted to 'long double'.

  - If one operand is of type 'double', the other operand is converted to 'double'.

  - If one operand is of type 'float', the other operand is converted to 'float'.

- If the sub-expression contains no 'long double', 'double' or 'float' types, operands of type 'char' and 'short' are converted to 'int'.

- Finally, if one operand is of type 'long int', the other is converted to 'long int'.

This is a little abstract; an example should illustrate the process:

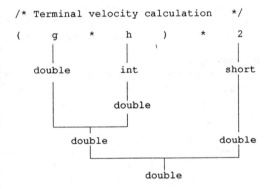

The final type of the expression is 'double'.

### Unsigned types

Type conversions involving operands of 'unsigned' type are dependent on the particular integer representation on a given system. While type conversion rules for all operands can be generalised with rules more complex than those given above, using type conversions on 'unsigned' operands produces nonportable code.

For example, if an 'unsigned short' is converted to an 'int', whether the resulting 'int' can hold a negative value depends on whether a 16-bit or 32-bit integer machine is in use.

### General principles
The following points should be noted:

- Whatever the type of an expression, the resultant value is converted to the type of the variable on the left-hand side of any assignment. If that variable is an 'int' and the type of the expression is a 'double', the conversion to 'int' will corrupt the value of the expression.

- Similarly, if an 'int' is converted to a 'char', information may be lost.

- It is very strongly advisable to ensure that the actual and formal parameters of a function are not only in the same order, but that their types are the same. A function returning, say, an 'int' to a 'char' in the calling function can cause unfortunate errors, including a program crash.

### The 'cast' operator
Type conversions may be forced in C by means of the unary 'cast' operator, which is a type specifier, enclosed in parentheses and prefixed to an expression.

The 'cast' may be used to avoid the consequences of unintended type conversions. In an expression such as that given in the terminal-velocity example above, type casting would look like this:

```
( g * (double)h ) * (double)2
```

This explicitly forces the type conversion according to the conversion rules given above. If 'int' h is assigned to a 'double', the value of h is converted by the assignment to 'double'. (double)h has the same effect.

- Explicit type conversion does not change the value of an expression like the one above, but is used for clarity.

- Type conversion can be vital. See the calculation of days_total in the function 'find_day' in the 'dates.c' program at the end of Chapter 5.

- Explicit type conversions are important for parameters in function calls and their specification in function prototypes.

Consider the 'atan' library function, which returns the arctangent of a double floating-point number. The function prototype is:

```
double atan(double);
```

From this, you can see that the function's return type is also 'double'. Consider this call to 'atan':

```
double    deg;
          .
          .
          .
deg = atan(1);
```

The argument, 1, is of type integer. With the above prototype, this is automatically converted to 'double', by the type cast in the prototype, before being used by 'atan'. The prototype could be written:

```
double atan();
```

This is legal but no type conversion would be done on the argument, 1, and 'atan' would return a garbage result to deg. To avoid this, the argument in the function call is type cast:

```
deg = atan((double)1);
```

The equivalent value in radians (0.78539...) of 45 degrees is assigned to deg.

The following expression:

```
5/7
```

gives 0, as a result of integer division. If this were not intended, you could use:

```
(float)5/(float)7
```

This gives the fractional result, .71428...

As a general rule, it is better to use variables in expressions which are, as far as possible, declared of the same type.

## Find the error

In each of the programs below, identify the line containing the error. Answers are given in Appendix C.

```
1    1    #define MASK      0x00001100
     2    #define TRUE      1
     3
     4    main()
     5
     6    {
     7    int x, device;
     8
     9    if (x & MASK == TRUE)
    10       {
    11       device++;
    12       comm_line_busy();
    13       }
    14    else
    15       process_data();
    16    }
```

```
2    1    #define MASK      0x00001100
     2    #define TRUE      1
     3
     4    main()
     5
     6    {
     7    int x, device;
     8
     9    if ((x & MASK) == TRUE)
    10       {
    11       device+;
    12       comm_line_busy();
    13       }
    14    else
    15       process_data();
    16    }
```

```
3   1   #define MASK      0x00001100
    2   #define TRUE      1
    3
    4   main()
    5
    6   {
    7   int x, device;
    8
    9   if ((x & MASK) == TRUE)
   10      {
   11      device++  = 1;
   12      comm_line_busy();
   13      }
   14   else
   15      process_data();
   16   }
```

```
4   1   int s;
    2   char stg[50];
    3
    4   /* initialise string */
    5
    6   stg[s] = '\0', s = 0;
```

# 5 Control Flow

## 5.1 Statement blocks

Previous chapters show that the body of a function following the function header is a compound statement or statement block.

C is a block-structured language. It encourages programs to be written according to the rather loosely-defined principles of 'structured programming'.

In the original definitions of languages such as COBOL and FORTRAN, there was no inherent structured approach. Change in the order of execution of statements in the program (control flow) was accomplished using an unconditional branch statement (GOTO) or a subroutine call (such as CALL, PERFORM).

Unstructured control flow makes for unreadable code. This is inefficient and more prone to programmer errors.

The following are some simple principles of the 'structured programming' approach:

- Programs are designed with a 'top down' approach; the major functions required for the solution are called from the highest-level function. Each of the called functions further refines the solution and calls further functions as necessary.

- Each function is short and carries out one logical task.

- Every function is as independent as possible of all other functions. Information should be exchanged between functions via parameters and return values. Use of global variables and shared code should be minimised.

- Unconditional branching should be avoided.

C provides the facilities necessary to meet these objectives. All statements are either simple statements

– expressions terminated by semicolons – or compound statements, which are statement groups enclosed by curly braces '{}'. A compound statement is syntactically equivalent to a simple statement.

Every C program must have a 'main' function from which, ideally, functions dealing with the highest level of the solution are called. It is sometimes held that no function should be longer than 50 lines of code; if it is, it should be broken down into a calling and one or more called functions.

By means of function return values and parameters, C allows exchange of data between functions to an extent which minimises use of global variables.

C provides a 'goto' statement for unconditional branching, but its use and power are severely restricted, as shown in Section 5.5.

C provides a range of statements for control of program execution flow. These are all based on switching control between the program's constituent compound statements and allow production of concise, logically-structured programs.

## 5.2   If

The general form of the 'if' statement is this:

```
if (<expression>)
    <statement1>
else
    <statement2>
```

The 'else' clause is optional.

The expression may be *any* legal expression, including an assignment, function call or arithmetic expression. The inherent boolean value of the expression determines change, if any, made to the program's flow of control by the 'if' statement.

The statements subject to the 'if' and the 'else' may be any legal single or compound statement. If a single statement is subject to an 'if' or 'else', use of

the compound-statement delimiters '{}' is optional;
for two or more statements they are necessary.

For example:

```
if ((c = getchar()) == 'q')
    {
    /* Finish program execution */
    printf ("Program execution terminating\n");
    return (0);
    }
```

'if' statements and the optional 'else' clauses may
be nested to arbitrary levels:

```
if (imm == 2)
    if (((iyy %4) != 0) || (iyy == MINYY))
        if (idd > MINFEB)
            return (FALSE);
```

This is one of the more complex tests in the example program, 'dates.c' (Figure 5.1, at the end of
this chapter). If the month is February AND (if the
year is not a leap year OR the year is 1900) AND if
the day is greater than 28, there is an error.

Each 'if' statement, including its subject compound
statement(s), is syntactically a single statement.
This is why the last example, although it contains
three nested 'if' statements, is a single statement;
no compound statement delimiters '{}' are necessary.

Delimiters could be used as follows:

```
if (imm == 2)
    {
    if (((iyy %4) != 0) || (iyy == MINYY))
        {
        if (idd > MINFEB)
            return (FALSE);
        }
    }
```

This makes no difference at all to the logic but gives
an improvement in code readability. Use of compound-statement braces becomes important when
the 'else' option is used.

```
if (imm == 2)
    if (((iyy %4) != 0) || (iyy == MINYY))
        if (idd > MINFEB)
            return (FALSE);
else
    return (TRUE);    /* valid date */
```

Each 'else' corresponds to the last 'if' statement for
which there is no other 'else', unless forced to correspond otherwise by means of '{}' braces.

In this example, the 'else' refers to the third 'if', although it is presumably intended to correspond
with the first. The following code is the minimum
required:

```
if (imm == 2)
    {
    if (((iyy %4) != 0) || (iyy == MINYY))
        if (idd > MINFEB)
            return (FALSE);
    }
else
    return (TRUE);    /* valid date */
```

Lastly, the whole 'if...else' construct may itself be
nested to arbitrary depth:

```
if (dd == 1)
    printf ("Monday\n");
else
if (dd == 2)
    printf ("Tuesday\n");
else
if (dd == 3)
    printf ("Wednesday\n");
else
if (dd == 4)
    printf ("Thursday\n");
else
if (dd == 5)
    printf ("Friday\n");
else
if (dd == 6)
    printf ("Saturday\n");
else
if (dd == 0)
```

```
    printf ("Sunday\n");
  else
    printf ("Error\n");
```

This is a multi-way decision. The construct is more efficient than it would be if all the 'if' statements were used without 'else' statements. As it stands, as soon as an individual test is successful, execution of the whole sequence stops. If dd is not in the 0-6 range, the last 'else' does processing for the 'none of the above' case and flags an error.

There is a special facility in C for more efficiently handling cases like this: the 'switch' statement in Section 5.6.

## 5.3  Loops: While, For and Do-While

Chapter 1 describes the basic rules governing these three loop types.

Here is another example of their use, this time from the 'dates.c' program. The first code sample uses the 'while' loop:

```
printf ("Press RETURN to start, 'q' and
                        RETURN to quit\n");

while ((c = getchar ()) != 'q')
    {
    /* call all the main functions of
       the program */
    printf ("Press RETURN to start, 'q'
                    and RETURN to quit\n");
    }
```

Next, the same thing in a 'for' loop:

```
for (
printf ("Press RETURN to start, 'q' and
        RETURN to quit\n"), c = getchar ();
c != 'q';
printf ("Press RETURN to start, 'q'
            and RETURN to quit\n"),
            c = getchar ()
    )
    {
```

```
    /* call all the main functions of the
       program */
}
```

Lastly, the code written with a 'do-while':

```
do
    {
    /* call all the main functions of the
       program */

    printf ("Press RETURN to start, 'q'
                      and RETURN to quit\n");
    } while ((c = getchar()) ! = 'q');
```

The requirements of this logic naturally suit use of the 'while' loop type. The 'for' loop works also, but is cumbersome because all the loop-controlling code and some unrelated prompt code must be grouped at the increment step at the top of the loop. It is best to restrict the increment step to loop-control code and put other statements into the body of the loop.

The 'do-while' variant does not produce the same result as the other two; no prompt precedes the first execution of the main functions.

The examples illustrate that, in most situations, one of the three loop types will be particularly suitable.

In general, the 'for' loop suits cases where the limits to the number of iterations are known in advance. This is the case in traversing an array with fixed subscript limits and in reading a data stream until end-of-file. Where the increment step code is lengthy, as in the case above, the 'for' loop is cumbersome.

It is always possible to use 'while' and 'for' interchangeably, but 'while' is usually suitable in those cases where 'for' is not.

The general form of the 'for' statement is:

```
for (<expr1>;<expr2>;<expr3>)
    <statement>
```

where *<expr1>* is the list of initialising expressions;
*<expr2>* is an expression list controlling loop termination; and *<expr3>* is the 'increment' step.

This is equivalent to:

```
<expr1>;
while (<expr2>)
    {
    <statement>
    <expr3>;
    }
```

The exception is when the 'continue' statement is
used; the 'continue' statement is dealt with in the
next section.

'do-while' is useful where it is required always to do
one iteration before the controlling condition is
tested. In the case above, this is not so and, although the code works, use of the 'do-while' is
inappropriate. Note that 'do-while' loop must be terminated with a semi-colon.

The two 'while' loop types must update the variable
whose value is controlling exit from the loop. The
variable is updated either in the loop's compound
statement or in the controlling expression. Care
needs to taken because the controlling expression
is evaluated in a different place in the two loop
types.

Finally, all three loop statements are syntactically
single statements. They may, therefore, be nested
to an arbitrary level without using compound statement delimiters:

```
for (i=0; i < 100 && arr1[i] != '\0';
    i++)
    for (j=0; j < 100 && arr2[j] != '\0';
        i++)
        if (arr1[i] == arr2[j])
            return (i);
```

The whole construct is a single statement.

Similar code is used in Section 5.5 to illustrate use
of the 'goto' statement, with compound statement
delimiters included for readability.

## 5.4 Break and Continue

It is sometimes necessary to exit a loop before the controlling condition causes the loop to end normally.

The 'break' and 'continue' statements, in different ways, allow this to happen.

### The 'break' statement

Let us define an character array of ten elements:

```
char arr[10];
```

Also define an array subscript:

```
int    sub;
```

We assume the array has been initialised with a null-terminated string. First, we traverse the array, print each character and exit the loop early on encountering the '\0' (null) character:

```
for (sub = 0; sub < 10; sub++)
    {
    if (arr[sub] == '\0')
       break;

    printf ("%c",arr[sub]);
    }
```

'break', when it is encountered, causes unconditional exit from the loop. Control is transferred to the first statement following the loop's compound statement. 'break' only causes exit from one level of loop; if the loops are nested, control is returned from the loop containing the 'break' to the outer loop.

'break' may be used within any of the loop types. It may only be used within loops or 'switch' statements.

### The 'continue' statement

'continue' may be illustrated using the same array and subscript counter defined above. Again, we want to traverse the array. If a newline character

'\n' is encountered, it is ignored and the characters, stripped of newlines, are printed.

```
sub = -1;
while (sub < 10)
    {
    sub++;
    if (arr[sub] == '\n')
        continue;
    printf ("%c",arr[sub]);
    }
```

'continue', when it is encountered, causes control to be passed to the loop's controlling expression or, in the case of a 'for' loop, the increment step. If the loop does not terminate naturally, the next iteration is performed. 'continue' has the effect of skipping at least part of the iteration of a loop.

'continue' may only be used within loop statements.

The example above illustrates well one of the dangers of using 'continue'. Because 'continue' causes part of an iteration to be skipped, problems arise if the loop-control variable is updated during the skipped part. In the case above, if sub were incremented after the 'printf' – as in ordinary code it probably would be – it would fail to be incremented for the first '\n' encountered. An infinite loop would result.

Although 'continue' may be used with any of the loop types, it is best suited to use with 'for' loops. This is because 'continue' returns control to the increment step, where loop-control operations are carried out.

## 5.5   Goto and labels

The unconditional branch instruction 'goto' may occasionally be useful but is never necessary. Anything that can be accomplished with 'goto' can also be done using combinations of the flow-control constructs already given.

The 'goto' statement is of the general form:

```
goto  <label>;
```

where *<label>* is an identifier conforming to the standard naming rules. Control is transferred unconditionally from the 'goto' statement to the point in the code where the named label followed by a colon ':' is encountered.

Use of 'goto' is not recommended; it tends to lead to undisciplined and unreadable code. However, there are a few cases where it serves a purpose.

'break' causes exit from one loop to the first statement in the code surrounding the loop. 'return' causes control to be returned from a function to the statement after the function call in the calling function. Where loops are nested two or more levels deep, there is no ready way to transfer control from the innermost loop to a point outside all the nested loops.

Here is an example of the use of 'goto'. Two character arrays are defined like this:

```
char arr1[100];
char arr2[100];
```

There are two subscript counters:

```
int i,j;
```

Assume the two arrays have been initialised with null-terminated strings. We want to find a character in arr2 which also exists in arr1 and then to exit.

```
for (i = 0; i < 100 && arr1[i] != '\0';
     i++)
   {
   for (j = 0; j < 100 && arr2[j] != '\0';
        j++)
      {
      if (arr1[i] == arr2[j])
         goto match;

      }
   }
printf ("No match found\n");

goto end;
```

```
match:    printf ("Match found %c\n",
                    arr1[i]);

end:      ;      /* null statement */
```

The 'goto' label only has scope within the function containing the 'goto' statement. 'goto' is therefore only valid within one function.

'goto' should not be used to transfer control to a statement within a loop. If the loop-control variables have already been initialised, use of 'goto' to a point in the middle of the loop may bypass that initialisation and the loop will go out of control, probably with unpleasant results.

## 5.6   Switch

As described above, C provides a statement to handle the special case of a multi-way decision. Here is the 'switch' implementation of the 'if...else...if' multi-way decision given earlier in this chapter.

```
switch (dd)
    {
    case 1:   printf ("Monday\n");
              break;
    case 2:   printf ("Tuesday\n");
              break;
    case 3:   printf ("Wednesday\n");
              break;
    case 4:   printf ("Thursday\n");
              break;
    case 5:   printf ("Friday\n");
              break;
    case 6:   printf ("Saturday\n");
              break;
    case 0:   printf ("Sunday\n");
              break;
    default:  printf ("Error\n");
              break;
    }
```

Control 'switches', depending on the variable dd. The variable must be of one of the integer types or of type 'char'. Each of the expected values of dd is enumerated. Zero or more statements are executed if dd is one of those values.

The 'case' values must be constant expressions.

All 'case' expressions in a given 'switch' statement must be unique.

'switch' is not an equivalent to the 'CASE' statements that are to be found in languages such as Pascal and PL/1. 'switch' in C merely provides entry points to a block of statements.

When control is transferred to a given entry point, execution starts at the first statement after that entry point. Unless directed otherwise, execution will simply fall through all code following, even though that code is associated with other 'case' entry points.

For this reason, it is necessary to insert a 'break' at the end of the statements subject to an entry point unless it is explicitly required that all the code following an entry point be executed.

In the example above, if all the 'break' statements were left out and dd had the value 3, control would fall through the 'switch' statement to the end and messages for all the days from Wednesday through to Sunday would be printed.

Omission of 'break' statements in a 'switch' can cause serious and unexpected errors.

'break' in a 'switch' causes control to be transferred completely out of the 'switch' statement.

'continue' does not apply to 'switch'; it will only have any effect if the 'switch' statement is embedded in a loop.

### The 'default' case

The 'default' case prefixes code which is executed if none of the previous case conditions is true. It is advisable, but not necessary, to end the statements subject to 'default' with a 'break'.

Inclusion of the 'default' case is optional. There may be only one 'default' in a switch statement. 'default' may occur anywhere in a 'switch' statement, but is usually placed at the end.

If the statements labelled by a 'case' immediately preceding the 'default' label are executed, control will fall through to the 'default' label unless a 'break' statement is encountered.

'switch' statements may be nested to arbitrary levels. A 'case' or 'default' label is part of the smallest 'switch' which contains it.

```c
/* Sample program 'dates.c': accepts as input a
   date of form dd/mm/yy, validates the date,
   and returns the result of the validation as
   well as the date's day-of-the-week.

   This program illustrates well most of the C
   constructs dealt with in the first five
   chapters. */

#include "stdio.h"
#include "stdlib.h"
#include "dates.h"   /* contains definitions of
                        symbolic constants and
                        global variables required
                        for this program       */

/* Function prototype declarations follow*/

int     get_data(char [], char [], char []);
int     validate(void);
int     find_day(void);
int     disp_day(int);

main ()

{
    /* define three small arrays for input of
       dates */
    char sdd[5], smm[5], syy[5];

    int c, dayofweek;

    printf ("Press RETURN to start, 'q' and
                            RETURN to quit\n");

    while ((c = getchar()) != 'q') /* quit on 'q' */
        {
        /* The 'get_data' function has as its
           formal parameters the three small date
           arrays. It initialises these arrays by
           accepting user input. It then converts
           the ASCII input to numeric data in the
           global variables idd, imm and iyy */
```

```
        get_data (sdd, smm, syy);

        /* The 'validate' function checks for
           wrong dates: e.g: 29/2/73, 32/5/64,
           24/-1/76. No parameters are passed to
           the function. It uses the global
           variables idd, imm and iyy which
           were initialised by 'get_data' and
           defined in the header file 'dates.h'*/

        if ((validate()) == FALSE)
           {
           printf ("Invalid Date Entered\n");
           break;
           }

        /* The 'find_day' function uses the global
           variables idd, imm, and iyy to
           compute the number of days elapsed
           between 1/1/1900 and the date entered
           by the user. The remainder after
           division of this number by 7 gives
           the displacement in the days of the
           week from 31/12/1899, which was a
           Sunday. The number of the day is
           returned as the function value.*/

        dayofweek = find_day ();

        /* The 'disp_day' function uses the
           integer  dayofweek as the parameter
           it uses to display the results.*/

        disp_day (dayofweek);
        printf ("Press RETURN to start,
                    'q' and RETURN to quit\n");
        }
}

int get_data (char dd[], char mm[], char yy[])

{
    printf ("Enter the day number: ");
    gets (dd);
    printf ("Enter the month number: ");
    gets (mm);
    printf ("Enter the year number: ");
    gets (yy);

    /* Convert the strings entered by the user
       to numeric */

    idd = atoi (dd);
    imm = atoi (mm);
    iyy = atoi (yy);
}
```

```c
int validate (void)

{

    /* Validate the date entered according to
       the well-known rules        */

    if ((iyy < MINYY) || (iyy > MAXYY))
        return (FALSE);
    if ((imm < MINMM) || (imm > MAXMM))
        return (FALSE);
    if ((idd < MINDD) || (idd > MAXDD))
        return (FALSE);
    if ((imm==4) || (imm==6) || (imm==9) || (imm==11))
        if (idd > (MAXDD - 1))
            return (FALSE);

    /* If the month is February and the year is
       divisible evenly by 4, we have a leap
       year, unless the year is 00. 1900 was not
       a leap year; 2000 will be. */

    if (imm == 2)
        {
        if (idd > MAXFEB)
            return (FALSE);
        if (((iyy % 4) != 0) || (iyy == MINYY))
            if (idd > MINFEB)
                return (FALSE);
        }
    /* If this point is reached, we return a
       valid date indicator */

    return (TRUE);
}

int find_day(void)

{
    short       no_leaps    = 0;
    short       yy_count    = 0;
    short       sub         = 1;
    long int    days_total  = 0;
    int         days_year   = 0;

    /* Count the number of leap years since 1900*/

    while (yy_count < iyy)
        {
        yy_count += 4;
        no_leaps++;
        }

    /* If the date entered is a leap year later
       than February and if it is not 1900, add
       1 to the total of leap years*/
```

```
    if ((yy_count == iyy) && (iyy != MINYY))
        if (imm > 2)
            no_leaps++;

    /* Calculate the number of days in the
       elapsed part of the year specified.*/

    while (sub < imm)
        {
        days_year += mdd[sub];
        sub++;
        }

    /* Compute the total number of days since
       1/1/1900   */

    days_total = (long)iyy * 365 + no_leaps
                 + days_year + idd;

    /* 1900 was not a leap year, so subtract 1
       from the leap-year total, unless the year
       entered was 00        */

    if (iyy != MINYY)
        days_total -= 1;

    /* 31/12/1899 was a Sunday and 1/1/1900 a
       Monday. The remainder after division by 7
       of the total number of days is therefore
       the day of the week where 1 is Monday, 2
       Tuesday ... 6 Saturday and 0 Sunday.*/

    return (days_total % 7);
}

int disp_day (int dd)

{
    switch (dd)
        {
        case 1:    printf ("%d/%d/%d valid,
                            Monday.\n",idd,imm,iyy);
                   break;
        case 2:    printf ("%d/%d/%d valid,
                            Tuesday.\n",idd,imm,iyy);
                   break;
        case 3:    printf ("%d/%d/%d valid,
                            Wednesday.\n",idd,imm,iyy);
                   break;
        case 4:    printf ("%d/%d/%d valid,
                            Thursday.\n",idd,imm,iyy);
                   break;
        case 5:    printf ("%d/%d/%d valid,
                            Friday.\n",idd,imm,iyy);
                   break;
        case 6:    printf ("%d/%d/%d valid,
                            Saturday.\n",idd,imm,iyy);
                   break;
```

```
    case 0:    printf ("%d/%d/%d valid,
                        Sunday.\n",idd,imm,iyy);
               break;
    default:   printf ("Cannot compute day of
                                    date\n");
               break;
    }
}
```

*Figure 5.1*

## Find the error

In each of the programs below, identify the line containing the error. Answers are given in Appendix C.

```
1   1   int c;
    2
    3   printf ("Enter data, 'q' to quit\n");
    4
    5   while ((c = getchar()) != 'q')
    6       {
    7       /* strip out all newlines from
                input */
    8
    9       if (c = '\n')
    10          break;
    11      printf ("%c\n",c);
    12      }

2   1   int c;
    2
    3   printf ("Enter data, 'q' to quit\n");
    4
    5   while ((c = getchar() != 'q')
    6       {
    7       /* strip out all newlines from
                input */
    8
    9       if (c == '\n')
    10          break;
```

```
     11      printf ("%c\n",c);
     12      }


3    1   int c;
     2
     3   printf ("Enter data, 'q' to quit\n");
     4
     5   while ((c = getchar()) != 'q');
     6      {
     7      /* strip out all newlines from
                input */
     8
     9      if (c == '\n')
     10         break;
     11      printf ("%c\n",c);
     12      }


4    1   int c;
     2
     3   printf ("Enter data, 'q' to quit\n");
     4
     5   goto print_msg;
     6
     7   while ((c = getchar()) != 'q')
     8      {
     9      /* strip out all newlines from
                input */
     10
     11      if (c == '\n')
     12         break;
     13
     14      print_msg: printf ("%c\n",c);
     15      }


5    1   #include "stdio.h"
     2
     3   main()
     4
     5   {
     6   int c;
     7
     8   printf ("Enter data, 'q' to quit\n");
     9
```

```
10 if ((c = getchar()) == 'q')
11    goto dont_start;
12 else
13    {
14    do
15        {
16        if (c == '\n')
17            break;
18        printf ("%c\n",c);
19        }
20    while ((c = getchar()) != 'q')
21    }
22 dont_start: ;
23 }
```

**6**
```
1  #include "stdio.h"
2
3  main ()
4
5  {
6  int c;
7
8  printf ("Enter data, 'q' to quit\n");
9
10 if ((c = getchar()) == 'q')
11    goto dont_start;
12 else
13    {
14    do
15        {
16        if (c == '\n')
17            break;
18        printf ("%c\n",c);
19        }
20    while ((c = getchar()) != 'q');
21    }
22 }
23
24 end_func ()
25
26 {
27 dont_start:   printf ("No data entered\n");
28 }
```

```
7    1    int season,sp,su,au,wi;
     2    int mm;
     3
     4    /* initialise season variables here */
     5
     6    switch (season)
     7        {
     8        case sp: mm = 2;
     9                 break;
     10       case su: mm = 5;
     11                break;
     12       case au: mm = 8;
     13                break;
     14       case wi: mm = 11;
     15                break;
     16       default: mm = 1;
     17                break;
     18       }
```

# 6 Arrays and Strings

## 6.1 Definition

Although arrays have been used in earlier chapters, they have not been dealt with in full and we have concentrated on use of the elementary data types.

Arrays cater for the case where many instances of a particular type of data object are being used. An array is a collection of contiguous data objects organised as a single entity.

All the data objects in an array are of the same size and type. Where it is necessary to mix in a single definition data objects of different sizes and types, structures are used. Structures are considered in Chapter 7.

Here is a definition of an array of data objects of type 'int':

```
int      numbers[10];
```

Ten integer data objects are defined. They are individually accessed by means of the identifier numbers suffixed by a *subscript* enclosed in square brackets '[]'.

| | |
|---|---|
| numbers[0] | is the first (element zero), 'leftmost' integer in the array |
| numbers[1] | is the second |
| . | |
| . | |
| . | |
| numbers[9] | is the last, or 'rightmost' |

Subscripts in C always start at zero and stop one short of the subscript limit given in the array definition.

It is easy to make a mistake like this:

```
int    i;
int    numbers[10];

for (i = 1; i <= 10; i++)
```

```
    {
    /*   do something with the array
         elements */
    }
```

The subscript counter i starts at 1 and finishes the
loop with value 10. numbers[10], however, is outside the bounds of the array as defined. The
compiler does no checking for errors such as this.
If, in the internal representation of the compiled
program, there is data immediately following the
array definition, it may be corrupted. It can be very
difficult to find array-bound errors; care is necessary.

Subscript values at the time of array definition
must be constants. C does not allow variable-bound
array definitions.

Arrays of objects of any data type may be defined:

```
char      charray[20];
float     flarray[50];
```

Both are legal examples.

It is also possible to define arrays of pointers and
arrays of aggregate data types, including arrays,
structures and other, programmer-defined data objects.

### Multi-dimensional arrays

Here is a definition of a multi-dimensional array –
an array of arrays:

```
int       matrix[20][15];
```

C is different in its syntax here to many other languages     in     that,     for     all     subscripts     of     a
multi-dimensional array, each subscript is individually enclosed in square brackets, both when
it is defined and when it is used.

Arrays may be defined of an arbitrary number of
dimensions. Most people find it intuitively difficult
to use arrays of more than three dimensions.

Considering the two-dimensional array, matrix,
above:

- There are 20 'rows', counted from zero to 19.

- There are 15 'columns', counted from zero to 14.

- `matrix[14][11]` can be thought of as the element at row 14, column 11.

- `matrix[14][11]` is more accurately thought of as the 11th element of array 14.

- The array `matrix` is not, in fact, organised in memory as a rectangle of integer data objects; it is a contiguous line of integers treated as 20 sets of 15 elements each.

- The subscripts of `matrix` are specified in row-column order – `matrix[r][c]` – and the 'column' subscript varies more rapidly than the 'row' subscript, in line with the way in which the array elements are stored in memory.

### Symbolic constants in array definitions

When arrays are being defined, it is very often a good thing to use symbolic constants like this:

```
#define   BAK_DOZ   13
      .
      .
      .
int       mdd[BAK_DOZ];
```

This defines an array (`mdd`) of type 'int', with 13 elements. In the program 'dates.c' (Figure 5.1), this array is there to hold the numbers of days in each of the months of the year. There are 13 elements so that subscript 0 may be unused and January to December can be indexed by the numbers 1 to 12.

Use of the symbolic constant instead of a 'magic number' such as 13 results in a better-documented program. It is also much easier – and less error-prone – to change all instances in the program of the subscript limit: only the original definition of the symbolic constant need be changed.

## 6.2 Initialisation

It is possible to initialise arrays with initialiser lists of constant data.

Both automatic and static arrays may be initialised in this way, but the results of initialisation for arrays of the two storage classes are different.

Most pre-ANSI standard compilers did not allow automatic arrays to be initialised as part of their definition. Many of these compilers are still in use, so care is needed to ensure that array initialisation code is portable.

For ANSI compilers, any initial values of 'auto' array elements that are not explicitly initialised are garbage; for static arrays, the array elements are zero. Static arrays are initialised at compile time; 'auto' arrays are initialised every time the function within which they are defined is called.

Array initialiser lists may be enclosed in curly braces, as in the example below, or may be a string literal enclosed by double quotes, an example of which is shown in the next section.

In the program 'dates.c', the global (implicitly static) array of integers mdd was defined and initialised like this:

```
int    mdd[13] = {0,31,28,31,30,31,30,31,
                  31,30,31,30,31};
```

The individual integer elements of the array were set (at compile time) to the values shown.

The data used to initialise an array must be a set of constant expressions enclosed in curly braces, separated by commas and terminated with a semi-colon.

Similarly, a character array might be defined and initialised like this:

```
char   arr[5] = {'h','e','l','l','o'};
```

If there are more initialising data objects within the curly braces than implied by the subscript limit, the compiler reports an error.

If there are fewer initialising data objects than the subscript limit, all excess elements in the array are set to zero for a static array, but have garbage values for an 'auto' array.

### Multi-dimensional arrays

Two- and multi-dimensional arrays are initialised as follows:

```
int    tab[3][4] = {   {1,2,3,4},
                       {5,6,7,8},
                       {9,10,11,12}
                   };
```

Here the outside curly braces are necessary; the internal ones are not but are included for readability.

Remember that the first array bound, [3], is the number of 'rows' and the second, [4], represents the number of 'columns'. Alternatively stated, tab consists of three four-element integer arrays.

In the above example:

```
tab[0][0]    == 1
tab[1][2]    == 7
tab[2][3]    == 12
```

### Omitted array bounds

Here, it is legal to omit one of the array bounds:

```
int    tab[][4] = {   {1,2,3,4},
                      {5,6,7,8},
                      {9,10,11,12}
                  };
```

The first array bound is inferred by the compiler on the basis of the initialisation. It is always illegal to omit the second array bound.

Where a one-dimensional array is being initialised, it is legal to leave out the array-bound limit. The compiler works out the number of array elements to allocate in memory based on the number of initialising data objects.

We have already seen that, where one or more arrays (addresses) are passed to a function as formal parameters, the declarations in the function header of the formal parameters look like this:

```
int get_data (char sdd[],char smm[],
     char syy[])
```

Given the empty array bounds for all three arrays, the compiler works out the space needed for each of the three internal variables sdd, smm and syy, based on the known size of the data being passed from the calling function.

## 6.3   Strings: terminated arrays

Strings are arrays of elements of type 'char' terminated by the first null character '\0' encountered in the array. There is no other difference between a string and an array of characters.

The definition from the last section:

```
char   arr[5] = {'h','e','l','l','o'};
```

is a character array; elements 0 to 4 of the array are initialised with the five letters of 'hello'.

The definition:

```
char arr[6] = {'h','e','l','l','o','\0'};
```

is a string initialised to 'hello' and null-terminated. Note that, to accommodate the null character, the second definition of arr needed one more element. Forgetting that the null character takes up one array element is a source of some difficult bugs.

The last definition is equivalent to:

```
char arr[6] = "hello";
```

Remember that a character constant, which can only be one character long, is delimited by single quotes as in 'a'. A string constant – also called a string literal – is delimited by double quotes. The double quotes imply the existence of a terminating null character.

| 'a' | is the ASCII numeric representation of the character a. |
|---|---|
| "a" | is a null-terminated string, equivalent to 'a','\0'. |

String literals may be used in the same way as variable strings. It is possible to get at individual characters of a string literal by suffixing the literal with a subscript:

```
"hello"[1]  ==  'e'
```

There is inefficiency in using string literals. Each time one is used, the compiler may allocate new memory space for it – an unnamed static array – even if it is identical to a string literal used earlier in the program.

By contrast, a variable array, once defined either externally or internally, will only have one memory allocation made for it at any given time.

If there is an error message like:

```
"Error: can't open file"
```

it is better from a standpoint of memory usage to initialise a variable string at definition time and repeatedly use the variable with 'printf' statements than it is to use the string literal throughout the program.

### Calculating string length
Figure 6.1 is an example string-handling program, which just calculates the length (counting from 1, not zero) of a string.

This is a very simple string-handling program, but there are several things to note about it.

The 'main' function is only given here for completeness; the actual string length calculation is done in the function 'slength'.

The function call to 'slength' is included as part of the second 'printf' statement in 'main'. Remember, every function has a return value and type. 'slength' is of type 'int', so the call to it is treated as an 'int' in the 'printf' statement.

```
#include "stdio.h"

int slength (char []);

main ()

{
    char        instring[50];

    printf ("Enter input string ");
    gets (instring);
    printf ("Length of string is %d",
            slength(instring));
}

int slength (char instring[])

{
    int i;

    for (i = 0; instring[i] != '\0'; i++)
        ;
    return (i);
}
```

*Figure 6.1*

'slength' does nothing but traverse the array until a null character is encountered, counting the number of characters on the way. The body of the 'for' loop doing this is just a semicolon, which is a null statement.

The counting of characters includes the null character '\0'. Normally, the null character is not included in a string's length. However, we want to report the string's length as if we were counting from 1, not zero. Counting in the null character compensates for the fact that we are counting from zero.

If the string is not terminated with a null character, 'slength' will run on until it reaches the end of the system's memory or it is stopped by the operating system. C does not check this for you and all kinds of interesting errors can result from omitting string terminators.

'slength' is equivalent to the standard library function 'strlen', the declaration of which is in the header file 'string.h'. 'strlen' is called in exactly the same way and with the same result as 'slength'.

### Finding a substring

The program in Figure 6.2 is an implementation of the PL/1 'substring' algorithm. There is no library function in C equivalent to the PL/1 built-in function 'SUBSTR'. The 'substr' function returns a part of a string specified by the start string address, and the start position and length of the substring required. The address of the substring is returned to the function calling 'substr'.

The 'main' function, again, is for completeness of the program; it initialises the input string and the start position and length of the required substring. It then calls the 'substr' function with these variables as parameters. The return type of 'substr' is a character pointer. 'substr' returns to the character pointer `cptr` in 'main' a pointer to the substring found and 'main' then prints the substring.

In the statement:

```
cptr = substr (stg, start, len);
```

`cptr` is a valid 'lvalue'; it is an expression referring to a memory location, the contents of which may be changed by the program.

An array name, on the other hand, is not a valid 'lvalue'. In the next section, this difference between an array name, which is the address of an array, and a character pointer to an array will be fully explained.

The 'substr' function first finds the length of the string from which it is to extract a substring. It does this by means of a call to the function 'slength', which is given above.

If the specified start position of the substring is greater than the length of the string, an error is flagged and a null string returned to 'main'.

The 'for' loop extracts the substring, which is then appended with a null character. The array name of the substring, which is its address, is returned to 'main'.

All the string-handling code in 'substr' is written using subscripts. In the next section, we shall see the pointer equivalents of both 'slength' and 'substr'.

Finally, as an example, assume that stg contains the string of characters "The quick brown fox":

```
cptr = substr (stg, 7, 5);
```

This will return to cptr a pointer to the string "ick b".

---

```
/* Program substr.c extracts from a string a
   substring specified by the substring's
   start position and length     */

#include "stdio.h"
#include "stdlib.h"
#define  MAX      50

char     sub[MAX];   /* global substring */

       /* function prototype declaration */
char *substr(char *, int, int);

main()
{
    char     stg[MAX],stgstart[5],stglen[5];
    char     *cptr;
    int      start,len;

    printf ("Enter string from which
                    substring will be taken ");

    /* Initialise array pointers to start of
       arrays */

    gets (stg);
    printf ("Enter start of substring ");
    gets (stgstart);
    printf ("Enter length of substring ");
    gets (stglen);
    start = atoi(stgstart);
    len   = atoi(stglen);
    if ((start <= 0) || (len < 0))
        {
        printf ("Invalid start or length\n");
        return (0);
        }
    cptr = substr (stg, start, len);
    printf ("Substring is %s\n",cptr);
}
```

```
char *substr(char stg[], int start, int len)

{
    int i, j;

    /* Find string length */

    i = slength(stg);
    if (start > i)
        {
        printf ("start %d > string length %d\n",
                start,i);
        sub[0] = '\0';
        return (sub);
        }
    start -= 1;         /*   allow for zero start
                             to array */

    for (i=start,j=0; i<start+len && stg[i]
            != '\0'; i++, j++)
        sub[j] = stg[i];
    sub[j] = '\0';

    return (sub);
}
```

*Figure 6.2*

## 6.4 Pointers to strings

Any array of a given type may be pointed to by a
pointer of the same type. For example, suppose that
an array of type 'int' is defined like this:

```
int       numbers[10];
```

An integer pointer is defined like this:

```
int       *iptr;
```

Then the pointer may be initialised to the start address of the array as follows:

```
iptr = numbers;
```

Now take the case of an array of type 'char' (see
Section 1.11):

```
char      instring[20];
char      *cptr;
```

These statements define a character array with 20 elements and a character pointer cptr.

cptr is initialised to the address of the character array like this:

```
cptr = instring;
```

Remember that *an array name is the address of its first element.*

The assignment above therefore initialises the character pointer cptr to the address of the start of the array instring.

*No '&' (address-of) operator is needed to access the address of an array.*

Where the '&' operator is applied to an array name, ANSI C yields the address of the address of the array.

The pointer cptr is now equivalent to the array address instring.

cptr is a valid 'lvalue' and may be assigned variable values. instring is not a valid 'lvalue' and assignments may not be made to it.

cptr may be thought of as a variable array address while instring is a static array address.

Consequently, the following (unrelated) statements are valid:

```
cptr++;
cptr = substr (stg, start, len);
```

These statements are not valid:

```
instring++;
instring = substr (stg, start, len);
```

In short, an array name must not be used on the left-hand side of an assignment or as the assignment operand of compound operators like '++'.

### Displacement calculations

When a subscripted array is used, the run-time system accesses, say, element number 27 by working out the displacement of element 27 from element zero (the base address) and setting up a

pointer to element 27. The programmer does not
see this, but every time a subscripted reference is
made to an array this calculation has to be performed.

Using pointers to the array, no base address displacement calculation has to be made. Therefore,
use of pointers to arrays is much more efficient
than subscripts, especially where intensive string
processing is concerned.

Given the following definitions:

```
char      stg[50];
char      *cptr, *lptr;
```

and initialising the pointers:

```
cptr = lptr = stg;
```

then this code finds the length of the string, assuming the string is initialised and null-terminated:

```
while (*lptr != '\0')
    lptr++;
return (lptr - cptr);
```

This is part of the pointer version of the 'slength'
function, which is given in full below.

Remember:

● cptr and lptr point at the address of the first
  element of character array stg

● *lptr is *the contents of* that element

● *lptr is the same as stg[0];

● lptr is the same as &stg[0]

When lptr is incremented by one, *lptr is the
same as stg[1]; when further incremented by one,
*lptr is the same as stg[2], and so on.

lptr is incremented until its contents (*lptr)
equal the null character. The displacement of the
pointer lptr from the array address stg (same as
cptr) may be calculated by subtraction, giving the
length of the string stg.

This is the first example we have seen of address arithmetic. The full rules of address arithmetic are given in Chapter 8.

## Pointers when calculating string length

Although use of pointers in string manipulation is more efficient than subscripts, there is one overhead: in a case such as 'slength', a displacement must be calculated which is the difference between the base address of the string and the final value of the character pointer. The need to calculate such displacements can make pointer code more cumbersome than its subscript equivalent, even though the pointer version is faster.

Figure 6.3 shows the pointer version of the 'slength' program in full.

```
#include "stdio.h"

int slength (char *);

main()

{
    char        instring[50];
    char        *cptr;

    /* Initialise the pointer to the
       string */

    cptr = instring;
    printf ("Enter input string ");
    gets (cptr);
    printf ("Length of string is %d",
                slength(cptr));
}

int slength (char *cptr)

{
    char *lptr; /* local character pointer */

    lptr = cptr;
    while (*lptr != '\0')
        lptr++;
    return (lptr - cptr);
}
```

*Figure 6.3*

The integer number returned by 'slength' to 'main' is the displacement between the two pointers lptr and cptr and is the length of the string instring.

The pointer implementation of 'substr' is given in Figure 6.4.

```c
/* Program substrp.c extracts from a string
   a substring specified by the substring's
   start position and length     */
#include "stdio.h"
#include "stdlib.h"
#define   MAX      50

char    sub[MAX];   /* global substring */

        /* function prototype declaration */
char *substr(char *, int, int);

main()
{
    char      stg[MAX],stgstart[5],stglen[5];
    char      *stgptr,*subptr;
    int       start,len;

    printf ("Enter string from which substring
                            will be taken ");

    /* Initialise array pointers to start of
       arrays */

    stgptr = stg;

    gets (stgptr);
    printf ("Enter start of substring ");
    gets (stgstart);
    printf ("Enter length of substring ");
    gets (stglen);
    start = atoi(stgstart);
    len   = atoi(stglen);
    if ((start <= 0) || (len < 0))
        {
        printf ("Invalid start or length\n");
        return (0);
        }
    subptr = substr (stgptr, start, len);
    printf ("Substring is %s\n",subptr);
}

char *substr(char *stgptr, int start, int len)

{
    char *cp1,*cp2,*cp3;
    short displ;
```

```
        displ = slength(stgptr);
        cp1 = stgptr;
        cp2 = sub;
        if (start > displ)
            {
            printf ("start %d > string length %d\n",
                start,displ);
            *cp2 = '\0';
            return (cp2);
            }
        start -= 1;       /*   allow for zero start
                                to array */

        for (cp1+=start,cp3=cp1; (cp1<cp3+len)&&
                (*cp1 != '\0'); cp1++,cp2++)
            *cp2 = *cp1;
        *cp2 = '\0';
        cp2 = sub;
        return (cp2);
    }
```

*Figure 6.4*

## Pointers when finding substrings

The pointer version of 'substr' is exactly equivalent to the one done with subscripts.

Character pointers are used in place of array names. The three local pointers in the 'substr' function – cp1, cp2 and cp3 – are used in place of the subscripts i and j.

● cp1 is used to traverse the string being searched.

● cp3 is fixed as the start of the substring in the string being searched.

● cp2 is used to point to the substring array.

The substring array sub is defined as a global variable. The reason for this is shown by a simplification:

```
    char *substr()

    {
        char      sub[MAX];
        char      *cp2;

        cp2 = sub;
        return (cp2);
    }
```

Suppose `sub` is defined as an automatic variable, local to the function 'substr'. There is a pointer, `cp2`, pointing to the array, returned to 'main'. In this case, upon return to 'main', `sub` is out of scope and has been destroyed. `cp2` is left pointing to something unpredictable.

This is a general pitfall for functions returning pointers to variables defined within the function.

There are several ways of avoiding the problem:

● Define the variable globally.

● Define the variable as a 'static' within the called function.

● Pass the variable as a parameter to the called function in the ordinary way and send back as the function's return value a pointer to the variable.

Taking the last of these and applying it to the simplified 'substr' function above:

```
char *substr(char *sub)

{
    char      *cp2;

    cp2 = sub;
    return (cp2);
}
```

`sub` is an array address which has been passed as a formal parameter to the function 'substr'. `sub` is an internal variable, but the array of which it is the address is now in scope for both 'substr' and the calling function. Returning from 'substr', the pointer `cp2` initialised to the array `sub` is now valid.

### Defining pointers to pointers

It is possible to define pointers at more than one level of indirection: to define a pointer to a pointer. The indirection may be arbitrarily complex, but more than two levels are never necessary.

This definition:

```
char *cptr[10];
```

creates an array of character pointers. It is *not* an array of characters or a string, but potentially an array of string addresses. Each of the pointers in the array must be initialised to an array or string before being used.

An array of string pointers is an alternative way of implementing a two-dimensional array of strings.

You could use subscripts to traverse the array of pointers like this:

```
cptr[4]   /* the fifth character pointer */
```

Instead, a pointer to the array of pointers may be used. For this we need to define a 'pointer to a pointer to a character':

```
char **cpp;
```

It must be initialised to the array of pointers like this:

```
cpp = cptr;
```

Now cpp is *a pointer to the first character pointer in the array*. *cpp is the first pointer in the array. **cpp is the 'object at' that first pointer.

## 6.5  Common string library functions

Many operations on strings, such as copying them, checking their length and comparing them, need to be carried out regularly. A standard header file, called 'string.h', is provided which allows us to use C's standard string library functions.

To use 'string.h', it should be included in the program in the ordinary way:

```
#include "string.h"
```

Here, we shall see a few important examples from the string library. Full lists of the available functions are given in Chapter 9 and Appendix A.

These are some of the most often-used functions:

| **strlen** | Finds the length of a string |
| **strcat** | Joins two strings |
| **strcpy** | Copies one string to another |
| **strcmp** | Compares two strings |
| **strncmp** | Compares parts of two strings |

We have already seen 'strlen':

```
int    len;
char   s[50];

/* initialise string here  */

len = strlen(s);
```

After this code, `len` contains the number of characters in the string, not counting the terminating null character.

'strcat' concatenates two strings:

```
char s1[50], s2[50];

/* initialise strings here */

strcat (s1, s2);
```

This appends the string `s2` to the end of the string `s1`. It is the programmer's responsibility to ensure that `s1` is long enough to accommodate the joined strings.

'strcpy' copies the second string operand to the first, stopping after the null character has been copied. The example given below illustrates its use.

'strcmp' and 'strncmp' both compare two strings and return a negative, zero or positive value, depending on whether the first string is lexicographically less than, equal to or greater than the second.

```
char s1[50], s2[50];

strcpy (s1, "hello");
strcpy (s2, "hallo");

result = strcmp(s1, s2);

/* s1 greater than s2, so result is positive */
```

'strncmp' does the same thing as 'strcmp', but only compares a specified number of characters in the two strings:

```
strncmp (s1, s2, 1);
```

In the example above, this would compare only the first letters of the two strings and would return a zero value, denoting equality.

Note that it is illegal to compare two strings using the '==' equality operator. Each character in the two strings must be compared to its counterpart in the other string. The library functions 'strcmp' and 'strncmp' are provided for this purpose.

**Example – strings within strings**
The program in Figure 6.5 accepts as input two strings s1 and s2 and finds the start position in s1 of s2. If s2 is not found in s1, a negative value is returned.

The 'strpos' function, which finds the position of s2 in s1 if there is a match, is an extremely useful function, particularly in text-processing applications such as text search/replace.

```
/* Program strpos.c -- finds position
   of string  s2  in s1. Returns position if
   found, negative value if not found.    */
#include "stdio.h"
#include "string.h"
#define MAX 50

int strpos (char *, char *);

main()
{
    char     str1[MAX], str2[MAX];
    char     *s1, *s2;
    int      pos;

    s1 = str1;
    s2 = str2;
    printf ("Enter string to be searched ");
    gets (s1);
    printf ("Enter search string ");
    gets (s2);
    pos = strpos (s1, s2);
    if (pos < 0)
        printf ("%s not found in %s", s2, s1);
```

```
    else
        printf ("%s at position %d in %s",
                s2,pos,s1);
}

int strpos (char *s1, char *s2)

{
    int     len;
    char    *lptr;  /* local char pointer */

    len  = strlen(s2);
    lptr = s1;

    while (*lptr != '\0')
        {
        if ((strncmp (lptr, s2, len)) == 0)
            return (lptr - s1 + 1);
        lptr++;
        }
    return (-1);
}
```

*Figure 6.5*

## Find the error

In each of the programs below, identify the line containing the error. Answers are given in Appendix C.

```
1   1   main ()
    2   {
    3       char instring[50], *cptr;
    4
    5       printf ("Enter the input string ");
    6       gets (instring);
    7
    8       /* Find string length */
    9
    10      while (*cptr != NULL)
    11          cptr++;
    12
    13      printf ("String length is %d ",
                    cptr - instring);
    14 }
```

```
2    1    main()
     2    {
     3        char instring[5] = "abcde";
     4        char *cptr = instring;
     5
     6        /* Find string length */
     7
     8        while (*cptr != NULL)
     9            cptr++;
     10
     11       printf ("String length is %d ",
                       cptr - instring);
     12   }
```

```
3    1    char instring[50] = {'a','b','c',
                                'd','e','f' };
     2
     3    main()
     4    {
     5        char *cptr = instring;
     6
     7        /* Find string length */
     8
     9        while (*cptr != NULL)
     10           cptr++;
     11
     12       printf ("String length is %d ",
                       cptr - instring);
     13   }
```

```
4    1    char instring[50] = {'a','b','c',
                                'd','e','f','\0' };
     2
     3    main()
     4    {
     5        char *cptr = instring;
     6        char outstring[50];
     7
     8        /* Find string length */
     9
     10       while (*cptr != NULL)
     11           cptr++;
     12
     13       /* Copy string to output */
```

```
14
15     outstring = instring;
16
17     printf ("String length is %d ",
                  cptr - instring);
18 }
```

**5**
```
1   char instring[50] = {'a','b','c',
                          'd','e','f','\0'};

2

3   main()
4   {
5       char *cptr = instring;
6
7
8       /* Find string length */
9
10      while (instring != NULL)
11          instring++;
12
13      printf ("String length is %d ",
                    instring - cptr);
14 }
```

# 7 Structures and Unions

The elements of an array are all the same size and type. If it is required to group together in one entity data objects of different sizes and types, *structures* are used. The *union* is a special case of the structure and is much more rarely used.

## 7.1 Structure basics

A structure is an aggregate data type: a collection of variables referenced under one name. The structure is also the first example we have seen of a programmer-defined data type.

### Structure declarations
Structures are of the general form:

```
struct <structure tag>
{
    <type-specifier1> <member1>;
    <type-specifier2> <member2>;
        .
        .
    <type-specifierN> <memberN>;
} <variable list>;
```

Here is an example of a structure declaration:

```
struct stock_type
{
    char    item_name[30];
    char    part_number[10];
    double  cost_price;
    double  sell_price;
    int     stock_on_hand;
    int     reorder_level;
};
```

Either the structure tag or the variable list may be omitted, but not both.

**Structure definitions**

The structure declaration above is not a definition – no memory space is allocated for the data objects specified.

All that now exists is the new, programmer-defined data type 'struct stock_type'. This is a template of data objects which may be used to define structure variables.

To define a structure variable the following form is used:

```
struct stock_type
{
    char     item_name[30];
    char     part_number[10];
    double   cost_price;
    double   sell_price;
    int      stock_on_hand;
    int      reorder_level;
} stock_item;
```

Now, we have *defined* an *instance* of the data type 'struct stock_type', for which memory is allocated and which is called stock_item.

Many instances of 'struct stock_type' may be defined like this:

```
struct stock_type
{
    char     item_name[30];
    char     part_number[10];
    double   cost_price;
    double   sell_price;
    int      stock_on_hand;
    int      reorder_level;
} stock_item1, stock_item2, stock_item3;
```

There is a better way of defining instances of a structure. For example:

```
struct stock_type stock_item1;
```

This separates the *declaration* of the structure from its *definition*. It allows the programmer to put the structure declaration in a '#include' file and later to define instances of that declaration in the program.

It is also possible to leave out the structure tag:

```
struct
{
    char       item_name[30];
    char       part_number[10];
    double     cost_price;
    double     sell_price;
    int        stock_on_hand;
    int        reorder_level;
}stock_item1, stock_item2, stock_item3;
```

In this case three instances of the structure are created and are given the names in the variable list. The disadvantage is that no further definitions of the structure may be made later in the program code. Without a tag, the structure's declaration cannot be referred to and definitions are not possible.

### Structure members

The typical way of defining a structure is as we have already seen:

```
struct stock_type stock_item1;
```

The component data objects of the structure are called *members*. In this example, there are six members of the structure and every instance of the structure will have the same six members.

To refer to an individual structure member, this is the syntax:

```
stock_item1.cost_price
```

The 'dot' or 'member of' operator references `cost_price` as a member of `stock_item1`, which is defined as an instance of the structure type 'struct stock_type'.

It is legal to have an array as a member of a structure. The fifth element of the array `item_name` is accessed like this:

```
stock_item1.item_name[4]
```

A structure may have one or more members which are also structures. A structure must not contain an instance of itself.

It is legal to assign to a structure another structure of identical type. This has been implemented in the ANSI C standard, but was not allowed by many earlier compilers.

It is illegal to compare two structures using the equality operator '=='. Each of the structure members must be individually compared.

## Nested structures

Here is an example of nested structures:

```
struct bin
{
    char        building[50];
    int         floor;
    int         bay;
    int         shelf;
    int         quantity;
};

struct detail
{
    int         height;
    int         width;
    int         depth;
    struct bin bin_loc;
    char        special_reqs[50];
    char        part_number[10];
};

struct stock_type
{
    char        item_name[30];
    char        part_number[10];
    struct detail item_detail;
    double      cost_price;
    double      sell_price;
    int         stock_on_hand;
    int         reorder_level;
};

struct stock_type stock_item;
```

The structure item_detail is nested within stock_item and contains further information about the stock item. The structure bin_loc is in turn nested within `item_detail` and holds information about a bin location.

The height of a particular item may be found thus:

```
stock_item.item_detail.height
```

The shelf on which that item is stored is:

```
stock_item.item_detail.bin_loc.shelf
```

The three nested structures above are declared and defined in reverse order. This is necessary to conform with C's scope rules for declarations of variables. The declaration of 'struct detail' is in scope for the definition of 'item_detail' because the declaration is made first. If the declaration of 'struct detail' were instead to follow that of 'struct stock_type', a compiler error would result, flagging 'struct detail' as being an unknown type.

Note that a member name or a structure tag of a structure may be used either in other structures or as the identifier for an elementary data object, without any clash. In the example above, uniqueness of the identifier `part_number` is ensured by the fact that it must be suffixed to a structure name by the dot operator like this:

```
stock_item.part_number
```

or:

```
stock_item.item_detail.part_number
```

Figure 7.1 is a simple program which initialises a structure of type 'struct stock_type' and prints out the contents.

---

```
#include "stdio.h"

double atof (const char *);

main()
{
    struct stock_type
        {
        char      item_name[30];
        char      part_number[10];
        double cost_price;
        double sell_price;
        int    stock_on_hand;
```

```
          int     reorder_level;
        };

    struct stock_type stock_item;
    char       instring[50];

    printf ("Enter item name _");
    gets (stock_item.item_name);
    printf ("Enter part number ");
    gets (stock_item.part_number);
    printf ("Enter cost price ");
    gets (instring);
    stock_item.cost_price = atof(instring);
    printf ("Enter selling price ");
    gets (instring);
    stock_item.sell_price = atof(instring);
    printf ("Enter stock on hand ");
    gets (instring);
    stock_item.stock_on_hand =
        atoi(instring);
    printf ("Enter reorder level ");
    gets (instring);
    stock_item.reorder_level =
        atoi(instring);

    printf ("%s",stock_item.item_name);
    printf ("%s",stock_item.part_number);
    printf ("%f",stock_item.cost_price);
    printf ("%f",stock_item.sell_price);
    printf ("%d",stock_item.stock_on_hand);
    printf ("%d",stock_item.reorder_level);
}
```

*Figure 7.1*

## 7.2 Arrays of structures

Structures may be grouped in arrays in the same way as any other data object.

Consider the declaration of the structure 'struct bin' in the last section:

```
struct bin
{
    char       building[50];
    int        floor;
    int        bay;
    int        shelf;
    int        quantity;
};
```

There are probably many bin locations where a given item is stored, perhaps dispersed among different buildings. Each bin location might be numbered up to a maximum. All the bin location detail could be held in an array of structures of type 'struct bin':

```
#define        BMAX   20 /* Maximum number of
                              locations at which
                              a part may be held*/
struct bin bin_arr[BMAX];
```

In this way, 20 instances of the structure type 'struct bin' are defined in an array with subscript limits 0 to 19.

The following code searches for a bin which has one of the items in stock:

```
int i;

for (i=0; i < BMAX; i++)
    {
    if (bin_arr[i].quantity != 0)
        {
        /* Item found */
        printf ("Item stored at bay %d
                    shelf %d in building %s ",
            bin_arr[i].bay,
            bin_arr[i].shelf,
            bin_arr[i].building);

        /* Take one out of stock */
        bin_arr[i].quantity -= 1;
        break;
        }
    }
```

In general, arrays of structures conform to exactly the same rules as arrays of any other data type.

Arrays of structures may be multi-dimensional and arrays of structures may be nested within other structure arrays. Excessive complexity of array nesting, however, produces hard-to-read and often inefficient code.

Initialisation of structures, described later in Section 7.5, is very much the same procedure as we have already seen for array initialisation.

## 7.3 Pointers to structures

Pointers to structures may be defined as easily as pointers to elementary data objects, such as integers.

Suppose that an integer and an integer pointer are defined like this:

```
int      i;
int      *iptr;
```

The pointer is initialised to the address of the memory which has been allocated for the variable i, like this:

```
iptr = &i;
```

### The arrow operator

In a syntactically analogous way, a structure and a structure pointer can be defined as follows:

```
struct stock_type
    {
    char     item_name[30];
    char     part_number[10];
    double   cost_price;
    double   sell_price;
    int      stock_on_hand;
    int      reorder_level;
    };
struct stock_type stock_item;
struct stock_type *sptr;
```

The structure pointer sptr is initialised to the address stock_item:

```
sptr = &stock_item;
```

Using the pointer sptr rather than the structure name stock_item, the structure members are accessed using a different syntax to the 'dot' operator, described above.

**The arrow operator is used like this:**

```
sptr->part_number      /* the array
                          part_number */

sptr->part_number[5]  /* element 6 of the
                          array part_number*/

sptr->stock_on_hand   /* the integer
                          stock_on_hand */
```

**With the pointer** sptr **initialised to the address of the structure** stock_item,

```
sptr-><member>
```

**is the same as:**

```
(*sptr).<member>
```

**Consider the following definitions:**

```
struct detail
{
    int       height;
    int       width;
    int       depth;
    char      special_reqs[50];
    char      part_number[10];
};

struct stock_type
{
    char      item_name[30];
    char      part_number[10];
    struct detail item_detail;
    struct detail *dptr;
    double    cost_price;
    double    sell_price;
    int       stock_on_hand;
    int       reorder_level;
};

struct stock_type stock_item;
struct stock_type *sptr;

/* Initialise structure pointers */

sptr =  &stock_item;
sptr->dptr = &sptr->item_detail;
```

Then:

```
stock_item.part_number   ==
    sptr->part_number

stock_item.item_name[8] ==
    sptr->item_name[8]

stock_item.cost_price    ==
    (*sptr).cost_price

stock_item                   ==   *sptr
```

Consider the nested structure item_detail:

```
stock_item.item_detail.part_number
```

This is equivalent to:

```
sptr->dptr->part_number;
```

As with all pointers, the structure pointers sptr and dptr do not point anywhere sensible or contain any data until they are initialised to the address of a data object for which memory has been allocated. It is an error to use uninitialised pointers.

In the code above the pointers are initialised to the addresses of the structure definitions stock_item and item_detail. The initialisation of sptr could have been done more concisely like this:

```
struct stock_type *sptr = &stock_item;
```

**Arrays of structure pointers**

It is possible to define arrays of pointers to structures like this:

```
struct stock_type *sptr[10];
```

This definition gives an array of ten elements, each of which is a pointer to a structure of type 'struct stock_type'. Before they can be sensibly used, they must be initialised to the addresses of defined structures.

There is nothing wrong with a pointer to an array of structure pointers:

```
/* Pointer to pointer to 'struct
   stock_type' */

struct stock_type **spp;
```

The pointer can be initiliased like this:

```
spp = sptr;
```

If this is confusing, remember that sptr is an array of pointers of type 'struct stock_type'. The address of that pointer array is, therefore, sptr. Note that spp is initialised to the address of the array of pointers. *spp *is the first pointer in the array.* **spp is the 'object at' that pointer.

## 7.4   Structures and functions

Structure pointers are used for two main purposes.

First, they are used to pass structures as parameters between functions. Structures are often very large, with a large amount of memory allocated to them. There is a significant overhead in copying large structures as parameters between functions, especially if the called function(s) are heavily used.

Second, pointers to structures are used for the construction of dynamically linked lists, which are described in Chapter 8.

### Passing structure pointers as parameters

Until the ANSI definition of the C language, many compilers prohibited passing structures as parameters between functions because of this overhead. These compilers required that a pointer to a structure, rather than the structure itself, be passed as the parameter.

Although ANSI C compilers allow the structure itself to be copied as a parameter, it is still often better to pass a structure pointer.

To pass a structure pointer as a parameter is a case of passing a parameter by reference, or *call by reference*. Another case of call by reference is when an array is used as a parameter between functions. In the case of an array, the array name is itself the address of the array and does not refer to the memory allocated for the array.

*Call by value*, which is the process of copying parameters between functions, is explained in Chapter 3. Call by reference was also referred to in Chapter 3. We have now seen two instances of call by reference; the full rules are given in Chapter 8.

To illustrate, consider a somewhat re-organised version of the program given in Figure 7.1. This is shown in Figure 7.2.

```c
#include "stdio.h"

struct stock_type
    {
    char    item_name[30];
    char    part_number[10];
    double cost_price;
    double sell_price;
    int    stock_on_hand;
    int    reorder_level;
    };

    double atof (const char *);
    void print_stock (struct stock_type *);

main ()
{
    struct stock_type stock_item;
    char        instring[50];
    printf ("Enter item name ");
    gets (stock_item.item_name);
    printf ("Enter part number ");
    gets (stock_item.part_number);
    printf ("Enter cost price ");
    gets (instring);
    stock_item.cost_price =
        atof(instring);
    printf ("Enter selling price ");
    gets (instring);
    stock_item.sell_price =
        atof(instring);
    printf ("Enter stock on hand ");
    gets (instring);
    stock_item.stock_on_hand =
        atoi(instring);
    printf ("Enter reorder level ");
    gets (instring);
    stock_item.reorder_level =
        atoi(instring);
```

```
    /* Call function to print structure
       data */

    print_stock (&stock_item);
}

void print_stock (struct stock_type
                  *sptr)
{
    printf ("%s",sptr->item_name);
    printf ("%s",sptr->part_number);
    printf ("%f",sptr->cost_price);
    printf ("%f",sptr->sell_price);
    printf ("%d",sptr->stock_on_hand);
    printf ("%d",sptr->reorder_level);
}
```

*Figure 7.2*

This is functionally equivalent to the earlier program. The difference is that the address of the structure stock_item is passed as a parameter to the function 'print_stock' and the formal parameter sptr is then used as a pointer to refer to the structure members for printing.

It could be done differently: having declared the structure as a global structure type then, within 'main', a structure pointer could be declared:

```
    struct item_type *sptr;
```

To initialise the pointer:

```
    sptr = &stock_item;
```

sptr would then be used in 'main' with arrow operators to initialise all the structure members and the function called as follows:

```
    stock_print (sptr);
```

### Passing structures as parameters

Up to now we have only passed the address of a pointer to a structure as a parameter between functions. With ANSI C compilers, it is possible to pass the structure itself. Consider the last part of the example program given above:

```
    /*   Pass the structure to 'print_stock'
         here rather than a pointer to the
         structure   */

print_stock (stock_item);
}

void print_stock (struct stock_type
                   sitem)

{
printf ("%s",sitem.item_name);
printf ("%s",sitem.part_number);
printf ("%f",sitem.cost_price);
printf ("%f",sitem.sell_price);
printf ("%d",sitem.stock_on_hand);
printf ("%d",sitem.reorder_level);
}
```

The code has been rewritten so that the actual data of the structure, stock_item, is *copied* in a call by value to the function 'print_stock'. The data is copied into the formal parameter sitem, which is then used in the ordinary way, referencing its members using the 'dot' operator.

It is almost always more efficient to pass large data objects, such as arrays and structures, as parameters between functions, using their addresses, rather than copying the whole structure. Copying structures between functions can result in significant overhead as member data of the structure is repeatedly 'pushed' and 'popped' in the system's stack space, which is used for transfer of parameters.

### Returning structures from functions

Finally, any function may have a return type which is a structure (or a pointer to a structure), in the same way that its return type might be 'double' or 'char *'.

To illustrate, we will modify the example program yet again (Figure 7.3). Here the structure stock_item is returned (copied) to ret_item in the calling function. It is only useful to do this if the structure's data has been changed in the called function.

```c
#include "stdio.h"

/* Function prototypes for functions
   returning non-integer variables */

double atof (const char *);
struct stock_type print_stock (struct
   stock_type);

struct stock_type
   {
   char     item_name[30];
   char     part_number[10];
   double cost_price;
   double sell_price;
   int    stock_on_hand;
   int    reorder_level;
   };

main ()
{
   struct stock_type stock_item, ret_item;
   char        instring[50];

   /* Initialise structure here        */

   /* Call function to print structure
      data */

   ret_item = print_stock (stock_item);
}

struct stock_type print_stock (struct
   stock_type stock_item)

{
printf ("%s",stock_item.item_name);
printf ("%s",stock_item.part_number);
printf ("%f",stock_item.cost_price);
printf ("%f",stock_item.sell_price);
printf ("%d",stock_item.stock_on_hand);
printf ("%d",stock_item.reorder_level);

return (stock_item);
}
```

*Figure 7.3*

## 7.5  Structure initialisation

Initialising a structure is like initialising an array.

Most pre-ANSI standard compilers did not allow automatic structures or automatic arrays of structures to be initialised as part of their definition. Many of these compilers are still in use, so care is needed to ensure that structure initialisation code is portable.

For ANSI compilers, any initial values of 'auto' structure members that are not explicitly initialised are garbage; for static structures, they are zero. Static structures are initialised at compile time; 'auto' structures are initialised every time the function within which they are defined is called.

Using the familiar declaration and definition of `stock_type` and `stock_item`, here is how `stock_item` is initialised:

```
struct stock_type
    {
    char      item_name[30];
    char      part_number[10];
    double    cost_price;
    double    sell_price;
    int       stock_on_hand;
    int       reorder_level;
    };
struct stock_type stock_item =

    {"Turbocharged sewing machine",
     "8705145B",
     275.65,
     340.00,
     50,
     20
    };
```

All the initialising expressions should be of the same types as the corresponding structure members, otherwise unpredictable things will happen.

Similarly, the initialising string constants should be shorter than the sizes of the array members of the structure to allow inclusion of the null character as terminator.

If there are too few expressions between the curly braces to initialise all the structure members, the uninitialised structure members are set to zero.

An array of these structures is initialised like this:

```
struct stock_type stock_item[] =

{   {"Turbocharged sewing machine",
     "8705145B",
     275.65,
     340.00,
     50,
     20
    },
    {"Economy sewing machine",
     "8705145A",
     150.00,
     199.99,
     100,
     30
    }
};
```

Only two elements of the array of structures are initialised. The array bounds are calculated by the compiler, depending on the number of initialising elements. If the array bound were explicitly given as, say, stock_item[10] then, in this case, the last eight elements would be zero-filled. If initialising data were provided for eleven or more elements, a compiler error reporting 'too many initialisers' would be generated.

Lastly, it is illegal to leave out the subscript limits from arrays that are members of structures being initialised. In order to initialise the structure, the compiler or run-time system has to be able to calculate the size of the structure, which it cannot do if the array bounds are undefined.

## 7.6 Bit fields

We have already seen how to do some bit-level manipulation operations using the bitwise operators. Chapter 10 completes the rules for 'bit twiddling' operations.

There is another way which C provides to do operations on single bits within a byte. It is based on a special use of structures and, although it is more cumbersome than using the bitwise operators, some people find it simpler.

A bit field is a special type of structure which defines how long, in bits, each member of the structure is to be.

The general form of a bit field structure is this:

```
struct <structure tag>
{
    <type specifier 1> <name 1> : <length 1>;
    <type specifier 2> <name 2> : <length 2>;
        .
        .
        .
    <type specifier N> <name N> : <length N>;
};
```

Taking the communications software example from Chapter 4 and reworking it, we have:

```
struct comm_states
{
    unsigned int dev_tx    : 1;
    unsigned int dev_rx    : 1;
    unsigned int dev_wait  : 1;
    unsigned int buf_full  : 1;
};

struct comm_states state_flag;
```

The variable state_flags contains four one-bit fields. The individual fields may be more than one bit.

The total of the lengths in bits of the members must not exceed the length in bits of the standard integer size on the system in use. This makes the use of bit fields machine-dependent and implies problems of portability for any software using them.

The members of a bit field may only be defined as type 'int' and should be further qualified as 'signed' or 'unsigned'. One-bit fields should be qualified 'unsigned' because a single bit cannot have a sign.

Bit field members are not aligned on word or byte boundaries and must not be used with pointer or address operators. Usage of the fields is as might be expected:

```
if (state_flag.dev_rx == 1)
    {
    printf ("comms device receiving data\n");
    disable_tx();
    }
```

Bit fields do not have to be named but may be used to 'pad out' unwanted bits:

```
struct comm_states
{
    unsigned int dev_tx     : 1;
    unsigned int dev_rx     : 1;
    unsigned int dev_wait   : 1;
    unsigned int buf_full   : 1;
    unsigned                : 6;
    unsigned int dev_hunt   : 1;
};
```

This might be declared if the six bits before the flag giving device hunt-mode status were unused.

Finally, members of a structure which are bit fields may be mixed with non-bit field members:

```
struct device
{
    char        dev_addr[3];
    int         rx_bufsiz;
    int         tx_bufsiz;
    struct comm_states state;
    unsigned    dev_mode : 3;
};
struct device i8274;
```

## 7.7 Unions

The syntax of a union is like that of a structure, but its meaning is different: at any given time it only holds one piece of data.

A structure is an aggregate data object which may hold several pieces of data of different types simultaneously. The declaration of a union may specify many data objects of various types, but only one of the data objects exists at any one time.

For a structure definition, the compiler allocates the total amount of memory space required by the sum of its members' sizes, plus any necessary space for word- or byte-alignment of the members. For a union, the compiler allocates the amount of memory space required by its largest individual member.

The following principles apply to unions:

● The syntax of a union is the same as that of a structure except that the keyword 'struct' is replaced by 'union'.

● All aspects of declaration and definition of a union are the same as for a structure.

● It is legal to have pointers to unions in the same way as for structures. Both the 'dot' and 'arrow' operators are used to access members of unions, depending on whether the actual definition of the union or a pointer to the union is used for access.

● Pointers to unions may be passed as parameters between functions.

● A union may only be initialised with data of the type of its first member.

● Unions may be nested within unions and structures. Unions may also occur in arrays and arrays in unions.

Figure 7.4 is a simple example of declaration, definition and use of a union. This program accepts as input a string. Some very rudimentary analysis is done on the string to determine whether the contents of the string represent an integer, a double floating-point number or a string.

Depending on the type of the data, it is copied to the appropriate member of the union, printed and then 'stored'.

A data structure such as this might be the basis of the definition of a spreadsheet cell. For a spreadsheet application, however, the validation and parsing of the data would have to be much more comprehensive. Information would also have to be stored concerning reference to other cells and the order of evaluation of the cells.

Note that the size of memory allocated to the union is the size of its largest member: the character array sval.

Data for only one member exists at any instant; as soon as, say, dval is initialised to a floating-point number, any previous data stored in the union is lost.

No track is kept of the type of data stored in a union; it is up to the programmer to know this.

```c
#include "stdio.h"
#include "stdlib.h"
#include "string.h"

char    analyse (char *);

/* Declare a union: it could be a simple
   spreadsheet cell */

union sp_cell

{
    int     ival;
    double  dval;
    char    sval[20];
};

main()
{
    char    instring[20], datatype;
    union sp_cell cell;
```

```
      printf ("Enter a number, fraction or
                                    string: ");
      gets (instring);
      datatype = analyse (instring);
      switch (datatype)
          {
          case 'i': cell.ival = atoi (instring);
                    printf ("Integer %d: ",
                              cell.ival);
                    break;
          case 'd': cell.dval = atof (instring);
                    printf ("Double %f: ",
                              cell.dval);
                    break;
          case 's': strcpy (cell.sval, instring);
                    printf ("String %s: ",
                              cell.sval);
                    break;
          default:  printf ("Invalid data\n");
                    break;
          }
      printf ("Data has been stored\n");
}

char analyse (char instring[])

{
      int i = 0;

      while ((instring[i] != '\0') && (i < 20))
          {
          if (instring[i] == '.')  /* decimal
                                      point */
              return ('d');
          if ((instring[i] < '0') ||
              (instring[i] > '9'))
              return ('s');
          i++;
          }
      return ('i');
}
```

*Figure 7.4*

## 7.8   Sizeof operator

The 'sizeof' operator is used when it is needed to know the size in bytes or characters in memory occupied by a data object.

A byte is nearly always the same in size as a 'char', but the equivalence is machine-dependent and there are sometimes cases where this is not so.

As we have already seen, the sizes of other data objects – 'float', 'int' and so on – are machine-dependent and no assumptions should be made about them when writing portable code.

Usually, it is not of interest to the programmer to know the actual number of bytes occupied by a particular data object. The data object simply occupies a certain amount of space and this information is used by another part of the program, while remaining transparent to the programmer.

The 'sizeof' operator returns the size in bytes of its operand. If the operand is a type-specifier, it must be enclosed in parentheses; if it is a variable, the parentheses are optional. 'sizeof' is used like this:

```
sizeof <variable name>;
sizeof (<type specifier>);
```

Some examples:

```
char    c;
int     i;
double  d;
float   f;
char    carr[10];
int     iarr[5];
char    *cptr;
int     *iptr = iarr;

sizeof (c)    /* == 1 by definition    */
sizeof (i)    /* == 4 if 32-bit system */
sizeof (d)    /* == 8 if 32-bit system */
sizeof (f)    /* == 4 if 32-bit system */
sizeof (carr) /* == 10 */
sizeof (iarr) /* == 20 if 32-bit system*/
```

```
sizeof (cptr)   /* implementation
                   dependent */
sizeof (iptr)   /* implementation
                   dependent */

sizeof (int)    /* == 4 if 32-bit system*/
sizeof (char)   /* == 1 by definition  */
sizeof (float)  /* == 4 if 32-bit system*/
sizeof (double) /* == 8 if 32-bit system*/
```

Suppose that we declare a simple structure and union like this:

```
struct sp_cell_s
{
    int      ival;
    double   dval;
    char     sval[20];
};
union sp_cell_u
{
    int      ival;
    double   dval;
    char     sval[20];
};
```

Then

```
sizeof (struct sp_cell_s)
```

will return 32, assuming a 4-byte integer, an 8-byte 'double' and adding the 20-byte array, plus the total bytes, if any, needed for member alignment.

```
sizeof (union sp_cell_u)
```

returns 20, because that is the size of the union's largest member.

'sizeof' is classed as a C operator, but a number of points should be made about it:

● It is more like a built-in function; if thought of as such, it is the only one in the C language.

● If the operand of 'sizeof' is an array name, then, as an exception, the array name is treated not as the address of the array but as representing the actual memory occupied by the array.

- The result of 'sizeof' is usually treated as an integer but is, in fact, an unsigned integer of type 'size_t', which is defined in the standard header file 'stddef.h'.

'sizeof' is mainly used where it is necessary for the program to dynamically allocate memory space to a data object and to determine buffer sizes for file I/O. Dynamic memory allocation is covered in Chapter 8 and file I/O in Chapter 9.

## 7.9  Linked structures

A structure must not contain a nested instance of itself, but it may contain a pointer to a data object of the same type. This fact is central to the construction of lists of structures linked by pointers.

Linked lists of structures are the main alternative to arrays as a method of storing many aggregate data objects of the same type: we can define arrays of structures and linked lists of structures.

Construction and use of linked lists is treated in full in Chapter 8; for now, here is an example of a structure declaration containing a pointer to another structure of the same type:

```
struct tnode
{
    int       x;
    double    y;
    struct tnode *next;
};
```

next is a pointer to a data object of type 'struct tnode'. Let us define two instances of this structure:

```
struct tnode first, second;
```

Initialise the structure members as follows:

```
first.x  = 5;
first.y  = 34.78;
second.x = 6;
second.y = 45.89;
```

The structures can be linked like this:

```
first.next = &second;
```

Now next points to the address of the second structure and the structures' members can be accessed like this:

```
first.x          /* == 5    */
first.y          /* == 34.78 */
second.x         /* == 6    */
second.y         /* == 45.89 */
first.next->x    /* == 6    */
first.next->y    /* == 45.89 */
second.next      /* indeterminate value,
                    should be set to NULL */
```

Suppose that we define a pointer to a structure of type 'struct tnode':

```
struct tnode *tptr;
```

Now initialise the pointer to the address of the structure first:

```
tptr = &first;
```

Then the members of the two structures are accessed like this:

```
tptr->x          /* == 5    */
tptr->y          /* == 34.78 */
tptr->next->x    /* == 6    */
tptr->next->y    /* == 45.89 */
```

A full program for building a linked list is given in Chapter 8.

## 7.10 Programmer-defined data types

As we have seen, use of structures allows the programmer to define a data type which is a combination or aggregate of C's basic data types.

So far, four storage class specifiers have been given:

```
auto        extern
static      register
```

There is a fifth, 'typedef', which allows the programmer to define original data types of arbitary complexity.

'typedef' fits uneasily as a member of C's storage class specifiers. It is really a method by which new type specifiers may be defined in terms of existing types.

Let us again consider the structure declaration 'struct stock_type':

```
struct stock_type
    {
    char       item_name[30];
    char       part_number[10];
    double     cost_price;
    double     sell_price;
    int        stock_on_hand;
    int        reorder_level;
    };
```

To illustrate a trivial case of using 'typedef' to define a new type, assume that all prices are stored as double floating-point numbers. We can then make the following definition:

```
typedef double price;
```

Finally define:

```
price cost_price;
price sell_price;
```

### Complex definitions

The example above serves no real purpose other than, perhaps, to improve program readability. We are interested in more complex definitions.

```
typedef struct stock_type
    {
    char       item_name[30];
    char       part_number[10];
    double     cost_price;
    double     sell_price;
    int        stock_on_hand;
    int        reorder_level;
    }stock_item;
```

In this case, stock_item is not a definition of an instance of the structure type 'struct stock_type', as it has been up to now. stock_item instead defines as a data type the structure type 'struct stock_type'. Now we can define instances of the structure as:

```
stock_item item1, item2;
```

Using the self-referencing structure declaration given in Section 7.9:

```
typedef struct tnode
{
    int      x;
    double   y;
    struct tnode *next;
}NODE;
```

NODE is now a data type specifying the structure type 'struct tnode'. To define two of these structures and a structure pointer:

```
NODE first, second, *tptr;

tptr = &first;
```

tptr may be used as in Section 7.9 to reference the members of the two structures.

Another use of 'typedef', which some programmers favour, is this:

```
typedef char *charptr;
```

Now charptr is a synonym for 'char *' and may be used to define character pointers:

```
charptr cptr1, cptr2;
```

'typedef', as well as being a way of defining new types, is a useful shorthand. Type definitions made using 'typedef' are usually grouped in include files at the top of the program and used throughout the program as a type specifier like any other.

'typedef' can also be useful in producing portable programs; 'short', 'int' or 'long' variable definitions which are part of a 'typedef' need only to changed in the 'typedef' when a program is being moved to a new system.

If the definition of the type changes, only one change to the include files is necessary; changes in the program text may not be needed.

In the example program given in Chapter 8 for building linked lists, 'typedef' is used as shown above.

## Find the error

In each of the programs below, identify the line containing the error. Answers are given in Appendix C.

```
1   1    struct emp_rec
    2    {
    3       char          emp_name[30];
    4       char          emp_addr[50];
    5       char          emp_no[10];
    6       double        emp_salary;
    7       double        emp_tfa;
    8    };
    9
    10  main ()
    11  {
    12      struct  emp_rec;
    13      char    instring[20];
    14      double atof (const char *);
    15
    16      /* Initialise structure */
    17
    18      printf ("Enter employee name ");
    19      gets (emp_rec.emp_name);
    20      printf ("Enter employee address ");
    21      gets (emp_rec.emp_addr);
    22      printf ("Enter employee number ");
    23      gets (emp_rec.emp_no);
    24      printf ("Enter employee salary ");
    25      emp_rec.emp_salary =
    26          atof(gets(instring));
    26      printf ("Enter employee tax
                                    allowance ");
    27      emp_rec.emp_salary =
    28          atof(gets(instring));
```

```
   28
   29    /* Call an existing function to
                print structure contents */
   30
   31    print_emp_rec(&emp_rec);
   32 }
```

```
2   1   struct emp_rec
    2   {
    3       char        emp_name[30];
    4       char        emp_addr[50];
    5       char        emp_no[10];
    6       double      emp_salary;
    7       double      emp_tfa;
    8   }
    9
   10   main()
   11   {
   12       struct emp_rec emp;
   13       char    instring[20];
   14       double atof (const char *);
   15
   16       /* Initialise structure */
   17
   18       printf ("Enter employee name ");
   19       gets (emp.emp_name);
   20       printf ("Enter employee address ");
   21       gets (emp.emp_addr);
   22       printf ("Enter employee number ");
   23       gets (emp.emp_no);
   24       printf ("Enter employee salary ");
   25       emp.emp_salary =
               atof(gets(instring));
   26       printf ("Enter employee tax
                                allowance ");
   27       emp.emp_salary =
               atof(gets(instring));
   28
   29       /* Call an existing function to
                print structure contents */
   30
   31       print_emp_rec(emp);
   32   }
```

```
3   1   struct emp_rec
    2   {
    3      char          emp_name[30];
    4      char          emp_addr[50];
    5      char          emp_no[10];
    6      double        emp_salary;
    7      double        emp_tfa;
    8   };
    9
   10   main()
   11   {
   12      struct emp_rec emp, *empptr;
   13      char     instring[20];
   14      double atof (const char *);
   15
   16      /* Initialise structure */
   17
   18      empptr = &emp;
   19      printf ("Enter employee name ");
   20      gets (empptr.emp_name);
   21      printf ("Enter employee address ");
   22      gets (empptr.emp_addr);
   23      printf ("Enter employee number ");
   24      gets (empptr.emp_no);
   25      printf ("Enter employee salary ");
   26      empptr.emp_salary =
                atof(gets(instring));
   27      printf ("Enter employee tax
                              allowance ");
   28      empptr.emp_salary =
                atof(gets(instring));
   29
   30      /* Call an existing function to
                  print structure contents */
   31
   32      print_emp_rec(empptr);
   33   }


4   1   struct emp_rec
    2   {
    3      char          emp_name[30];
    4      char          emp_addr[50];
    5      char          emp_no[10];
    6      double        emp_salary;
```

```
 7      double      emp_tfa;
 8  };
 9
10  main()
11  {
12      struct emp_rec emp, *empptr;
13      char    instring[20];
14      double atof (const char *);
15
16      /* Initialise structure */
17
18      printf ("Enter employee name ");
19      gets (empptr->emp_name);
20      printf ("Enter employee address ");
21      gets (empptr->emp_addr);
22      printf ("Enter employee number ");
23      gets (empptr->emp_no);
24      printf ("Enter employee salary ");
25      empptr->emp_salary =
            atof(gets(instring));
26      printf ("Enter employee tax
                              allowance ");
27      empptr->emp_salary =
            atof(gets(instring));
28
29      /* Call an existing function to
               print structure contents */
30
31      print_emp_rec(empptr);
32  }
```

**5**
```
 1  struct emp_rec
 2  {
 3      char        emp_name[30];
 4      char        emp_addr[50];
 5      char        emp_no[10];
 6      double      emp_salary;
 7      double      emp_tfa;
 8      struct emp_rec next;
 9  };
10
11  main()
12  {
13      struct emp_rec emp, *empptr;
```

```
 14     char    instring[20];
 15     double atof (const char *);
 16
 17     /* Initialise structure */
 18
 19     empptr = &emp;
 20     printf ("Enter employee name ");
 21     gets (empptr->emp_name);
 22     printf ("Enter employee address ");
 23     gets (empptr->emp_addr);
 24     printf ("Enter employee number ");
 25     gets (empptr->emp_no);
 26     printf ("Enter employee salary ");
 27     empptr->emp_salary =
           atof(gets(instring));
 28     printf ("Enter employee tax
                              allowance ");
 29     empptr->emp_salary =
           atof(gets(instring));
 30
 31     /* Call an existing function to
              print structure contents */
 32
 33     print_emp_rec(empptr);
 34 }
```

```
6  1   typedef struct emp_rec
   2   {
   3       char        emp_name[30];
   4       char        emp_addr[50];
   5       char        emp_no[10];
   6       double      emp_salary;
   7       double      emp_tfa;
   8       struct emp_rec *next;
   9   }record;
  10
  11 main()
  12 {
  13     struct emp_rec record, *empptr;
  14     char    instring[20];
  15     double atof (const char *);
  16
  17     /* Initialise structure */
  18
```

```
19     empptr = &record;
20     printf ("Enter employee name ");
21     gets (empptr->emp_name);
22     printf ("Enter employee address ");
23     gets (empptr->emp_addr);
24     printf ("Enter employee number ");
25     gets (empptr->emp_no);
26     printf ("Enter employee salary ");
27     empptr->emp_salary =
           atof(gets(instring));
28     printf ("Enter employee tax
                               allowance ");
29     empptr->emp_salary =
           atof(gets(instring));
30
31     /* Call an existing function to
              print structure contents */
32
33     print_emp_rec(empptr);
34 }
```

```
7   1   struct device_flag
    2   {
    3       unsigned int dev_busy:       1;
    4       unsigned int minor_device:   3;
    5       double sync_rate:            7;
    6       unsigned int stat_flags:     4;
    7   };
```

# 8 Pointers in Depth

## 8.1 Pointers and addresses

The actual low-level implementation of C pointers on a given system is dependent on the machine's architecture and operating system.

In general, however, a typical computer system has an area of memory available to user programs. This is organised as a large number of machine words, made up in turn of a number of (usually 8-bit) bytes. The byte is the smallest addressable unit of memory. In the context of implementations of the C language, a byte is usually equivalent to the data type 'char'.

We are not concerned here with the machine-dependent aspects of pointer implementations but rather with the uniform interface which is presented to programmers by the ANSI-standard C language definition. It is enough to think of a C pointer as closely corresponding to a system memory address. Pointers may then be used to 'chain' the storage at these addresses to produce, for example, linked structures.

It is important to note that if pointers to different data types are defined, the internal implementation of the pointers is different for every type. It is therefore a serious mistake, for example, to assign the address of a 'float' variable to an integer pointer or to perform address arithmetic on pointers of different types.

One of the main benefits of using pointers in C is that pointers are equivalent to absolute memory addresses: using pointers, there is no need in array operations, for example, to perform base-address displacement calculations every time a pointer element is accessed. This fact makes pointers more efficient and faster for operations with complex data types than array subscripting.

A pointer is an address: no memory is allocated for it by the compiler other than the memory required to store that address. It is always an error to use a pointer which has not been initialised to the address of a data object to which memory has been allocated.

### Pointer syntax

The syntax for definition and use of pointers deserves some comment. The '*' is the *indirection* or *dereferencing* operator. Its use is equivalent to address-indirection techniques used in many assembler languages. It is used in both the definition of pointers and in dereferencing the content of the location pointed to.

The simplest type of pointer, the character pointer, is defined and initialised like this:

```
char      c;
char      *cptr = &c;
```

The 'contents of' or 'object at' the variable c is later dereferenced with:

```
*cptr
```

But the uses of '*cptr' in the two cases mean different things and the difference is not always made clear in standard references.

- 'char *cptr' means '(char *)cptr' or 'char* cptr'.

- 'char *' is the type specifier for 'character pointer'.

The '*' operator in the definition is associated with the 'char' type specifier, not with the variable identifier; code as usually written does not reflect this.

The whole definition means:

> Define a variable cptr which is a 'char *' – a pointer to a data object of type 'char'

'*cptr' used outside the pointer's definition *is* a unit. The dereferencing operator '*' is associated with the variable identifier cptr and means:

> Return the object at the address referenced by the pointer cptr

## 8.2 Pointers to data objects

Any simple or complex data object which may be defined in C, including a pointer, may have a corresponding pointer defined for it.

Here is the general form for definition of a pointer to a data object of a given type, for definition of an object of the same type and for the initialisation of the pointer:

```
<type-specifier> <variable-name>;
<type-specifier> *<pointer-name>;

<pointer-name> = &<variable-name>;
```

There is one notable exception to this rule: when the address of an array is being assigned to a pointer the 'address of' operator '&' is unnecessary. An array name is the array's address – except when the array name is used with the 'sizeof' operator, in which case the array name refers to the memory allocated for the array. These exceptions constitute what is probably the most serious inconsistency in the C language.

A function is not a variable but, as we shall see later in this chapter, pointers to functions may be, and regularly are, defined.

Here are some examples of pointer definitions and initialisations which illustrate the general form above:

```
/* Variable definitions and
   initialisation */

char      cval    = 'q';
int       ival    = 5;
float     fval    = 3.14;
double    dval    = 2.71828;
char      carr[50] = {'a','b','c','\0'};
int       iarr[20] = {1, 2, 3, 4, 5};

struct tnode
{
    int      x;
    double   y;
```

```
    struct tnode *next;
}NODE1,NODE2;

typedef struct tnode
{
    int      x;
    double   y;
    struct tnode *next;
}NODETYPE;

/* Pointer definitions */

char     *cptr;
int      *iptr;
float    *fptr;
double   *dptr;
struct tnode *tptr1;
NODETYPE *tptr2;

/* Pointer initialisation */

cptr = &cval;   /* *cptr == 'q' */

iptr = &ival;   /* *iptr == 5  */

fptr = &fval;   /* *fptr == 3.14 */

dptr = &dval;   /* *dptr == 2.71828*/

cptr = carr;    /* Note the exception!
                   *cptr == carr[0] == 'a'*/
iptr = iarr;    /* *iptr == iarr[0] == 1 */

tptr1 = &NODE1;/* *tptr1 == NODE1
                   structure data */

tptr2 = &NODE1;/* *tptr2 == same
                   structure data */

tptr2->x        /* contents of NODE1.x*/

tptr2->next = &NODE2;

tptr2->next->x /* contents of NODE2.x*/
```

## 8.3  Function call by reference

There are three ways of passing data between functions: by return value; passing parameters by
value; and passing parameters by reference.

The rules for the first two are given in Chapter 3 and many examples of their use have been shown.

The third method of passing parameters is known as *call by reference*. Call by reference means passing to another function *the address of a data object* rather than a copy of the actual data object itself. To copy the parameter is known as *call by value*. We have already seen two examples of call by reference.

Because the name of an array is the address of the array, to pass an array name as a parameter between functions is to pass the array's address, not the actual array data.

Although it is legal to pass a structure as a parameter by value, it is better to pass it by reference. This is done by passing as a parameter either a pointer to the structure or the name of the structure prefixed with the 'address of' operator '&'.

All other variables may be transferred as parameters between functions by reference: that is, by supplying their addresses or pointers as parameters.

There are two effective differences between call by value and call by reference:

● Call by value copies the parameter data to the called function. If the called function changes the data, the change to the copy is not reflected in the calling function.

  Call by reference only copies the address of the parameter data to the called function. Both the calling and called functions are looking at the same instance of the data; a change to the data by the called function will cause the data to be changed in the calling function also.

● Call by value means that data has to be copied between functions using the system's stack space. If large aggregate data objects like structures are copied and if the called function is intensively used, call by value is inefficient and will degrade program performance. Call by reference is never less efficient than call by value and is often much more so.

### Passing an integer by reference

Figure 8.1 includes an example of an integer being passed by reference to a called function.

The result from this program is:

```
Initial value 7
Changed value 14
```

Notice again that the address of the integer is passed to the function 'changei'. The called function's formal parameter, to which the integer address is passed, is an integer pointer.

To access or change the object at the pointer iptr requires use of the dereferencing operator '*'.

Call by reference can be done by passing a pointer to a variable instead of the variable's address, generated by use of the '&' operator. The result is identical. Figure 8.2 shows the modified program.

```
#include "stdio.h"

void changei (int *);

main()
{
    int i = 7;

    printf ("Initial value %d ",i);

    /* Pass the address of i as parameter */

    changei (&i);
    printf ("Changed value %d ",i);
}

void changei (int *iptr)
{
    *iptr = 14;
}
```

*Figure 8.1*

```
#include "stdio.h"

void changei (int *);

main()
{
    int i = 7;
    int *ip;

    ip = &i;
    printf ("Initial value %d ",*ip);

    /* Pass the address of i as parameter */

    changei (ip);
    printf ("Changed value %d ",*ip);
}

void changei (int *iptr)

{
    *iptr = 14;
}
```

*Figure 8.2*

## Passing a structure address by reference

The method of passing parameters by reference is
analogous for all other data objects except arrays.
Figure 8.3 includes an example using a structure
address as a parameter.

```
#include "stdio.h"

struct tnode
{
    int      x;
    double y;
    struct tnode *next;
};

void change_struct (struct tnode *);

main()
{
    struct tnode element;

    /* initialise structure members*/

    element.x    = 5;
    element.y    = 3.14;
    element.next = NULL;
    printf ("Structure elements %d %f ",
              element.x, element.y);
```

```
    change_struct (&element);

    printf ("Structure elements %d %f ",
                element.x, element.y);
}

void change_struct (struct tnode
                *element)

{
    element->x = 14;
    element->y = 6.28;
}
```

*Figure 8.3*

## Function call by reference

To illustrate function call by reference using arrays as parameters, consider the simple program in Figure 8.4, which changes all blanks in a string to newline characters.

```
#include "stdio.h"

void change_str (char *);

main()
{
    char instring[50];

    printf ("Enter a string ");
    gets (instring);
    change_str (instring);
    printf ("Changed string %s ", instring);
}

void change_str (char *cptr)

{
    while (*cptr != '\0')
        {
        if (*cptr == ' ')
            *cptr = '\n';
        cptr++;
        }
}
```

*Figure 8.4*

Notice how two idioms are mixed: an array name is passed from 'main' as a parameter to 'change_str'; the formal parameter in the called function is a character pointer. The contents of the string will be changed back in 'main' if it contains any blanks.

'main' could be written like this for identical behaviour:

```
#include "stdio.h"

void change_str (char *);

main ()
{
    char instring[50], *cp;

    cp = instring;
    printf ("Enter a string ");
    gets (cp);
    change_str (cp);
    printf ("Changed string %s ", cp);
}
```

### Passing a pointer to a pointer

In all the examples above the address of a data object is passed to the called function. Both the calling and called functions are handling the same instance of the data object and so any change to the data object is seen in both functions. The pointer or address of the object is not changed; the contents of the object itself are.

Sometimes, we may want to modify the pointer itself. In this case, we must pass as a parameter a pointer to the pointer.

Suppose in the last example program, we wanted to return from the function 'change_str' a pointer pointing to the first character in the string after the last blank. This involves changing the value of the array pointer as well as the array itself. The program is shown in Figure 8.5. If the string:

```
now is the time for all good men
```

is entered at the 'printf' prompt, the result will be:

```
men
```

```
#include "stdio.h"

void change_str (char **);

main()
{
    char instring[50], *cp;

    cp = instring;
    printf ("Enter a string ");
    gets (cp);

/*  Here pass a pointer to the array
    pointer to 'change_str'. The array
    pointer value will be changed as well
    as the array contents. The array will
    afterwards start at a different
    address. */

    change_str (&cp);
    printf ("Changed string %s ", cp);
}
void change_str (char **cptr)

{
    char        *lptr; /* local pointer */

    while (**cptr != '\0')
        {
        if (**cptr == ' ')
            {
            lptr = *cptr;
            **cptr = '\n';
            }
        (*cptr)++;
        }
    lptr++;
    *cptr = lptr;
}
```

*Figure 8.5*

The value of the pointer cp has been changed from the address of the start of instring to a new address further down the array.

The program itself is subtle and needs careful inspection. Note that the address of the pointer – &cp – is passed from 'main'. If just the pointer cp were passed, it would be dereferenced with a single '*' in the called function, and the value of the pointer cp in 'main' would not be changed. But, where the address of the pointer is sent, it must be dereferenced with two asterisks; change to the value of the pointer to instring will be reflected in 'main'. &cp – a pointer to a pointer – is passed as a parameter to 'change_str'. In 'change_str':

● The formal parameter must be of type 'char **', doubly dereferencing the pointer to a pointer, cptr.

● **cptr is the contents of the first element of the array instring.

● *cptr is the pointer to instring.

● cptr is the pointer to the pointer to instring.

It is widely regarded as a good thing that no deeper level of indirection is ever necessary in C.

## 8.4   Address arithmetic

Address arithmetic on pointers is possible and is usually used with pointers to arrays.

We have already seen a typical case of address arithmetic: where the displacement of a character pointer from its start point needs to be calculated in order to return a relative position in a string.

Also, we have become accustomed to repeatedly incrementing pointer values by one when traversing an array.

Let ptr be a pointer to an array of elements of some type. ptr++ increments the pointer to the next element in the array. *ptr is the contents of the element currently pointed to. ptr += n increments the pointer by the value of n array elements.

Each element of a character array is, by definition, one 'char' or byte long. It is reasonable to expect a pointer to such an array to be incremented by one to point to the next element.

In fact, for all arrays of any type of element, the 'increment by one' rule holds. The size of each element is automatically taken into account and it is a mistake, when incrementing the array pointer, to try to calculate the size of the array elements and increment by that amount.

To summarise: incrementing a pointer by one makes it point to the next element for all arrays, regardless of the type of the elements.

### Address arithmetic example

Consider the structure declaration 'struct stock_type' of Chapter 7:

```
struct stock_type
{
    char      item_name[30];
    char      part_number[10];
    double    cost_price;
    double    sell_price;
    int       stock_on_hand;
    int       reorder_level;
};
```

Now we define an array of these structures and initialise a pointer to the array:

```
struct stock_type stockarr[100];
struct stock_type *stockptr;
int    count;

stockptr = stockarr;
```

Even though each array element occupies at least 50 bytes on any system, the pointer need only be repeatedly incremented by one to traverse the array:

```
for (count = 0; count < 100;
count++,stockptr++)
    {
    /* Set the array elements zero or
       empty */

    stockptr->item_name[0]    = '\0';
    stockptr->part_number[0]  = '\0';
    stockptr->cost_price      = 0.0;
    stockptr->sell_price      = 0.0
    stockptr->stock_on_hand   = 0;
    stockptr->reorder_level   = 0;
    }
```

When two pointers to an array are subtracted, the result is not the number of bytes which separate the array elements but the number of array elements.

Arithmetic of this type should not be carried out on pointers of different types; the results will be unpredictable and probably catastrophic. Two pointers of the same type may be subtracted but not added, divided or multiplied. Addition to a pointer is only legal where the pointer is incremented by an integer value.

## Precedence and associativity

Care needs to be taken with the syntax of pointer increment and decrement operations.

The '++', '--' and '*' (dereferencing) operators are all of the same precedence and associate right-to-left.

As a result, some unexpected things can happen when these operators are mixed in the same expression. For example:

```
*ptr++
```

is a very common expression. It means that the object at ptr is fetched and then the pointer value is incremented by one. If we want to add one to the object at the pointer, we need:

```
(*ptr)++
```

Pointer arithmetic can easily get out of control, with very unpleasant results. Liberal use of parentheses in the case of mixed-operator expressions like that above and care about not mixing pointer types will save a lot of trouble. Figure 8.6 illustrates this point.

```
#include "stdio.h"

char stg[] = "nmlkjihgfedcba";

main ()
{
    char *ptr = stg;

    printf ("Initial string is %s\n",ptr);
    printf ("*ptr++ %c\n",*ptr++);
    printf ("*ptr %c\n",*ptr);
```

```
    printf ("Re-initialise pointer\n");
    ptr = stg;
    printf ("*(ptr++) %c\n",*(ptr++));
    printf ("*ptr %c\n",*ptr);

    printf ("Re-initialise pointer\n");
    ptr = stg;
    printf ("(*ptr)++ %c\n",(*ptr)++);
    printf ("*ptr %c\n",*ptr);

    printf ("Re-initialise pointer\n");
    ptr = stg;
    printf ("++*ptr %c\n", ++*ptr);
    printf ("*ptr %c\n", *ptr);

    printf ("Re-initialise pointer\n");
    ptr = stg;
    printf ("++(*ptr) %c\n", ++(*ptr));
    printf ("*ptr %c\n", *ptr);

    printf ("Re-initialise pointer\n");
    ptr = stg;
    printf ("*++ptr %c\n", *++ptr);
    printf ("*ptr %c\n", *ptr);

    printf ("re-initialise pointer\n");
    ptr = stg;
    printf ("*(++ptr) %c\n", *(++ptr));
    printf ("*ptr %c\n", *ptr);

    /* Results to be expected:

        *ptr++     n
        *ptr       m

        *(ptr++)   n
        *ptr       m

        (*ptr)++   n
        *ptr       o

        ++*ptr     p
        *ptr       p

        ++(*ptr)   q
        *ptr       q

        *++ptr     m
        *ptr       m

        *(++ptr)   m
        *ptr       m                     */
}
```

*Figure 8.6*

## 8.5   Pointers to functions

Consider an array of integers and an integer
pointer:

```
int        i[10];
int        *iptr;
```

We make `iptr` a pointer to the array of integers by
initialising it to the address of the array:

```
iptr = i;
```

C syntax allows definition of a pointer to the array
in a more concise form:

```
int        (*iptr)[10];
```

This also makes `iptr` a pointer to an array of integers.

Pointers to functions are defined with similar syntax.

Functions are not variables, but it is possible to
define pointers to them, store such pointers in arrays and pass them as parameters between
functions.

Function pointers are typically used in specific applications where outside events determine which of
many functions is to be called next. In such cases
an array of pointers to functions is often used to
control function calls.

A pointer to a function contains the internal
memory address of the entry point of that function.
The address of the function is obtained using only
the function's name.

Here is how to define a pointer to a function:

```
int (*fptr)();
```

`fptr` is a pointer to a function returning an 'int'.

Note that all the parentheses here are necessary.
For example:

```
int *fptr();
```

This is not a pointer to a function, but the definition of a function returning a pointer to an 'int'.

**Example – drawing horizontal lines**

Figure 8.7 is a simple example using pointers to functions.

```
#include "stdio.h"

int drawline (int);

main ()
{
    /* Define a pointer to a function
       with an 'int' as a parameter */
    int (*fptr) (int len);

    /* Assign a function address to the
       pointer */

    (*fptr) = drawline;

    (*fptr) (50);
}

int drawline (int len)
{
    while (len > 0)
        {
        printf ("-");
        len--;
        }
    printf ("\n");
}
```

*Figure 8.7*

The program draws horizontal lines. Use of the function pointer is not necessary; the function 'drawline' could as easily have been called explicitly.

fptr is defined as a function pointer. The name of the function 'drawline', which is the address of that function, is assigned to *fptr, which is then used as a function name exactly as 'drawline' could be.

During function pointer assignment, ANSI C also allows the '&' operator to be applied to a function name and makes the use of the dereferencing operator on the pointer optional:

```
(*fptr)  =    drawline;
(*fptr)  =   &drawline;
fptr     =    drawline;
fptr     =   &drawline;
```

These are all equivalent and give the same result.

The function call using the pointer may alternatively be made without explicit dereferencing:

```
fptr (50);
```

Let us look at a more complex construct:

```
int   (*fptr[])();
```

This is an array of pointers to functions returning 'int' values. Function pointers are often initialised in arrays.

### Example – communications
Figure 8.8 includes a highly simplified communications application.

```
#include "stdio.h"

/* Function prototypes */

int    idle(void), transmit(void),
       receive(void);

/* In a real communication software
   system, the following two variables
   would be defined globally and changed
   by external interrupts   */

int    tx_int, rx_int;

/* Initialise array of function pointers
   with function addresses       */

int    (*state_arr[])() = {idle,transmit,
       receive};

int state = 0;

main()
{
    /* Simulate communications state
       machine */

    while (1)     /* loop forever */
       {
       /* Initially, state == 0, call
          function zero (idle) first.
```

```
            Thereafter, call functions
            according to the state value
            returned by the last function.*/

        (*state_arr[state]) ();
        }
}

int idle (void)
{
    /* Wait until interrupt received */

    if (tx_int)
        state = 1;
    else
    if (rx_int)
        state = 2;
    else
        {
        printf ("System interrupt error\n");
        exit (0);
        }
}
int transmit (void)
{
    /* Dummy transmit */

    printf ("Buffer successfully transmitted.....");

    /* Set state to zero (idle) */

    state = 0;
}

int receive (void)
{
    /* Dummy receive */

    printf ("Buffer received....");

    /* Set state to zero (idle) */

    state = 0;
}
```

*Figure 8.8*

## 8.6   Arrays of pointers

As described above, for a called function to change the value of a pointer passed to it as a parameter, a pointer to the pointer must be supplied as a parameter.

Pointers may be arrayed like any other data type. An array of pointers is actually a pointer to several pointers.

In Section 6.4, an array of character pointers was defined:

```
char *cptr[10];
```

Each of the pointers in the array must be initialised to the address of an array of characters before being used:

```
char *cptr[10] = {"Now is the time\n",
                  "for all good men\n",
                  "to come to the aid\n",
                  "of the party\n"};
```

In this case, pointers zero to 3 of the ten-element pointer array are initialised to the addresses of the four literal strings shown within curly braces.

`cptr[2]` points to the string `"to come to the aid\n"`.

Instead of using subscripts, we may use a pointer to the array of pointers:

```
char **cpp;
```

Now cpp is initialised to the address of the array of pointers:

```
cpp = cptr;
```

Note the following points:

- `*cpp` points to the string `"Now is the time\n"`.

- `**cpp` is the first character in that string, 'N'.

- `(*cpp)++` increments the pointer to the first string; `**cpp` is now the second character, 'o'.

**Example of pointer arrays**

Figure 8.9 contains an example program which exercises many of the possible operations using a pointer to pointers on a two-dimensional character array. The array of pointers is defined and initialised to its five component strings outside 'main'.

Four main operations are done by the program. The first two are the same thing done with subscripts and pointers respectively. The iteration is terminated when the first character of a string pointed at by one of the array of pointers is NULL or '\0'. NULL is the same as '\0' and is provided as a symbolic constant in the standard header file.

The third operation prints only the first line of text, but does it repeatedly, dropping one character from the start each time. The increment step of the 'for' loop does this. *cpp is the pointer to the current string and is assigned to the temporary pointer cp. cp++ adds one to that pointer on each iteration, thereby skipping a character on the left of the text in each loop.

The fourth step, on the outside 'for' loop, accesses every text string in the array. The inner 'for' loop traverses each of those strings with the simple character pointer cp and prints out each character individually.

This program should be inspected carefully and understood because the methods of single and double indirection that it shows are generally applicable for all cases in C where arrays of pointers are used.

Let us again define an array of pointers to the structure stock_type:

```
struct stock_type *sptr[10];
```

If we assume that these pointers have been properly initialised, we can define a pointer to a pointer of type 'struct stock_type':

```
struct stock_type **spp;
```

Next, initialise the pointer to the array of pointers:

```
spp = sptr;
```

```c
#include "stdio.h"

char *cptr[] = {"Now is the time\n",
                "for all good men\n",
                "to come to the aid\n",
                "of the party.\n",""};
main ()
{
    char **cpp;    /* Pointer to array of
                      pointers */
    char *cp;      /* Pointer to string */
    char ans[5];
    int i;

    /* Print out all the strings using
       subscripts */

    printf ("Press RETURN to continue ");
    gets (ans);

    for (i = 0; *cptr[i] != NULL; i++)
       printf ("%s",cptr[i]);

    /* Now do the same, with pointers */

    printf ("Press RETURN to continue ");
    gets (ans);

    for (cpp = cptr; **cpp != NULL; cpp++)
       printf ("%s",*cpp);

    /* Now print the first line repeatedly,
       dropping one character from the front
       each time */

    printf ("Press RETURN to continue ");
    gets (ans);

    for (cpp = cptr, cp = *cpp; *cp != NULL;
         cp++)
       printf ("%s",cp);

    /* Finally, print each character in the
       array individually   */

    printf ("Press RETURN to continue ");
    gets (ans);

    for (cpp = cptr; **cpp != NULL; cpp++)
       for (cp = *cpp; *cp != NULL; cp++)
          printf (" %c",*cp);
}
```

*Figure 8.9*

We may now use spp and sptr in the same way as we used cpp and cptr, even though the types of objects pointed at are completely different.

● spp is the same as sptr and is the address of the array of pointers to structures.

● *spp is the first pointer in the array and points to the first structure.

● (*spp)++ causes *spp to point to the second structure.

● (*spp)->cost_price accesses the cost_price member of the structure pointed to by *spp. The parentheses around *spp are necessary because the 'arrow' operator '->' has higher precedence than the indirection operator '*'.

● **spp is the data of the structure pointed to.

● (**spp).cost_price is the cost_price member of that structure accessed using the 'dot' operator.

## 8.7  Complex pointer declarations

Even the most experienced C programmers can be confused by the notation of complex pointer declarations. When a certain level of indirection is reached, the notation is simply not intuitively easy to understand. More than two levels of indirection are never required and should be avoided.

Restricting the indirection to the maximum of two levels, here is a sequence of pointer declarations from the simplest to the most complex:

```
int    *i;       /* i  pointer to
                    integer */

int    *iptr[]; /* array of pointers to
                    integers */

int    **ipp;   /* pointer to pointer(s)
                    to integers */
int    *f();    /* function returning a
                    pointer to an 'int' */
```

```
int    (*ipp)[5];  /* pointer to an array
                      [5] of 'int'*/
int    (*f)();  /* pointer to function
                   returning an 'int'*/
int    (*f[])();    /* array of pointers to
                       functions returning
                       'int'    */
int    *(*f[])();  /* array of pointers to
                      functions returning
                      pointers to 'int's!! */
```

If a pointer is passed as a parameter to a function
and if any change made to it by the called function
is to be 'visible' in the calling function, a pointer to
the pointer is the parameter passed:

```
void chg_stg (char **);

main()
{
char *cptr;

    .
    .

chg_stg (&cptr);
    .
/* Changed value of pointer returned to
   here */
}

void chg_stg (char **cptr)

{
    .
    .

(*cptr)++;  /* Change the pointer's
               value */
}
```

## 8.8  Dynamic storage allocation

Up to now, the only way we have seen of allocating
memory space to a variable is by definition of that
variable and allocation of space by the compiler.

All variables defined up to this point have been of fixed length and the allocation of space has been outside the control of the programmer.

An array of structures is the best way we have so far seen of storing repeated instances of aggregate data, or 'records'. However, arrays themselves are of fixed length, determined at compile time.

If the records were being generated from data entered at a device such as a terminal, then no matter how large the array defined to store the data, it might not be large enough.

What is needed is a way of allocating memory, under the control of the programmer, at program run time. This is accomplished using a number of functions, the prototypes of which are available in the standard header file 'stdlib.h'.

The four functions are these:

**malloc**  Returns a pointer to a specified amount of memory, which is allocated from the program heap by the C dynamic allocation system.

**calloc**  Does the same as 'malloc', but returns a pointer to an array of allocated memory.

**realloc**  Changes the size of the allocated memory to a specified size.

**free**  Frees allocated memory and makes it available to the system heap.

Of these functions, only 'malloc' and 'free' are necessary to write programs which use dynamic allocation and it is these we shall concentrate on.

### The 'malloc' function
Consider the structure declaration:

```
typedef struct tnode
    {
    int     x;
    double  y;
    struct tnode *next;
    }NODE;
```

Remember that NODE is not a structure definition but, because of the use of 'typedef', is a new, programmer-defined type specifier which declares as a type a structure of type 'struct tnode'.

Let us allocate enough space for such a structure. To allocate the space, we need to know the size of the structure. We find this using the 'sizeof' operator:

```
sizeof(NODE)    /* returns structure size
                   in bytes    */
```

The memory allocation function 'malloc' takes one parameter, the size in bytes of the object for which memory is to be allocated. Memory for one instance of the structure is allocated like this:

```
malloc(sizeof(NODE))
```

'malloc' returns a pointer to the memory if the memory was successfully allocated, otherwise NULL. Therefore the return value from 'malloc' should be assigned to a pointer of the same type as the data object for which space is being allocated:

```
NODE *ptr1;
ptr1 = ((NODE *)malloc(sizeof(NODE)))
```

Here, the result of the 'malloc' operation is assigned to the pointer ptr1, which is a pointer to a structure of type NODE. 'malloc', however, returns a pointer of type 'void'. (In the pre-ANSI standard definition of C, 'malloc' returned a character pointer.)

The ANSI standard makes 'void *' the generic pointer type; in the original definition of the C language, the generic pointer type was 'char *'.

A 'void' pointer may be assigned to any pointer type without a type cast. Here, the return value of 'malloc' is nonetheless type-cast with 'NODE *' (pointer to NODE) and assigned to ptr1.

All other pointers in pointer assignments of mixed type must be type cast.

`ptr1` is now a pointer to an instance in memory of structure type NODE.

If there was insufficient memory available for the allocation, or if there were some other error, 'malloc' would return NULL to `ptr1`. This leads us to the complete construct for allocation of memory:

```
if ((ptr1 = ((NODE *)malloc
    (sizeof(NODE)))) == NULL)
    {
    printf ("Memory allocation error\n");
    exit (0);      /* Exit program */
    }
/* Memory successfully allocated */
```

'exit' is a library function, the prototype for which is in the header file 'stdlib.h'. It causes graceful program termination and returns a status code to the local operating system environment. Zero indicates a successful termination.

In general, the combination of 'malloc' and 'sizeof' may be used to allocate memory dynamically (at program run time) for any data object. The operand of 'sizeof' may be either an instance of the data object for which memory has already been assigned or the object's type specifier.

Notice that it is not necessary to know the size of the memory allocation. The result of 'sizeof' is just passed (transparently to the programmer) to 'malloc'.

### The 'free' function
If it is necessary to free the memory associated with a pointer by the 'malloc' function, the 'free' function is used:

```
free (ptr1);
```

This will usually be done after allocation of memory when that memory is to be discarded, for example when a list element is deleted.

## 8.9   Lists

The main alternative to the array for storing many instances of a particular data type is the *linked list*.

A linked list comprises a number of 'nodes' which are linked to each other by their respective memory addresses. Each node may have many links to other nodes; lists may be circular or arbitrarily complex.

Here we shall only deal with lists that are 'singly linked forward'.

Linked lists of this type must have a *list header*, a fixed pointer which always represents the start of the list. The list must be terminated with a NULL node. The list must not be circular in any part.

Each node in the list contains an address, which is the memory address of the next node in the list.

The result is a list comprising zero or more nodes. If there are one or more nodes, the list header pointer points to the first node, the pointer in the first node points to the second node, and so on.

### Inserting and deleting elements

Linked lists have different characteristics to arrays.

To delete or insert an element in an array is difficult and inefficient: when deleting, all the elements to the right must be 'shuffled' one position left; when inserting, all the elements to the right must be 'shuffled' one position right (if there is space) and the insertion made.

To insert or delete in a list is easy. Suppose we have a list with two elements, A and B. Suppose also that B is pointed to by A->next and that B->next points to NULL. We want to insert element C between A and B.

The operations necessary are these:

```
C->next = &(B)
A->next = &(C)
```

With two address assignments, we accomplish what, using arrays, might take several hundred assignments.

Relative to arrays, the disadvantages of lists are that operations on them are slower, and programmer error more frequent.

### Building a list

The structure 'struct tnode' is used with 'typedef' as the structure declaration which we will use in a full program to build a linked list.

```
typedef struct tnode
    {
    int     x;
    double  y;
    struct tnode *next;
    }NODE;
```

A list header pointer is defined also:

```
NODE    *lhdr;
```

These declarations are included in an original header file called 'list.h'.

Figure 8.10 shows the full program for building and printing a linked list.

```
/*
    list.h
                            */

typedef struct tnode
{
    int     x;
    double  y;
    struct tnode *next;
}NODE;

NODE *lhdr;

/*
            list.c
                        */

#include "stdio.h"
#include "stdlib.h"
#include "list.h"

main()
{
```

```
NODE *lptr1, *lptr2;
char istr[10], dstr[10];
int c;

/* Set header and all local pointers
   to NULL */

lptr1 = lptr2 = lhdr = NULL;

/* Data is entered and added to the list
   in a loop  */

printf ("type RETURN to add to list, 'q'
                            to quit. ");
while ((c = getchar()) != 'q')
   {
   /* Allocate memory space for a node */
   if ((lptr1 = ((NODE *)
       malloc(sizeof(NODE)))) == NULL)
       {
       printf ("Memory allocation error\n");
       exit(0);
       }

   /*      User enters data here    */

   printf ("Enter an integer: ");
   gets (istr);
   printf ("Enter a double: ");
   lptr1->x = atoi(istr);
   gets (dstr);
   lptr1->y = atof(dstr);

   /*      Add the element to the list */

   if (lhdr == NULL)
       lhdr = lptr1;
   else
       lptr2->next = lptr1;
   lptr2 = lptr1;
   lptr2->next = NULL;
   printf ("RETURN to add to the list,
                        'q' to quit\n");
   }
/*      Display the completed list      */

lptr1 = lhdr;
while (lptr1 != NULL)
   {
   printf ("Integer %d Double %f\n",
           lptr1->x, lptr1->y);
   lptr1 = lptr1->next;
   }
}        /* End of 'main' */
```

*Figure 8.10*

The program first defines two pointers of type NODE and two character arrays for data entry with 'gets'. It then sets all the pointers to NULL.

There are four main steps in the program, which are controlled by a 'while' loop depending on user input.

The first allocates space for a list node, as demonstrated in Section 8.8. The second step prompts the user to enter data to initialise the list node.

The third step adds the node to the list. If the list is null (i.e: has no members) then the list header pointer must be pointed to the newly allocated node as the list header. Otherwise the new node is added to the end of the existing list. The 'next' pointer within the new node is set to NULL.

Finally, when the user has finished entering data, the contents of all the list nodes are printed out.

Note that:

```
lptr1 = lptr1->next;
```

advances the pointer one node down the list each time it is executed.

## Find the error

In each of the programs below, identify the line containing the error. Answers are given in Appendix C.

```
1    1    main ()
     2    {
     3        char instring[50], *cptr;
     4        int  i = 0;
     5
     6        printf ("Enter input string\n");
     7        gets (instring);
     8
     9        while (*cptr++ != NULL)
```

```
10          i++;
11
12      printf ("Length of input string
                    is %d",i);
13 }
```

**2**
```
1   main ()
2   {
3       char instring[50], *cptr =
                            instring;
4       int  i = 0;
5
6       printf ("Enter input string\n");
7       gets (instring);
8
9       while (cptr++ != NULL)
10          i++;
11
12      printf ("Length of input string
                    is %d",i);
13 }
```

**3**
```
1   int *f()
2   {
3     int i = 14;
4
5     return &i;
6   }
```

**4**
```
1   main()
2   {
3       int i = 4;
4
5       printf ("Initial value is %d",i);
6       changei (&i);
7       printf ("Returned value is %d",i);
8   }
9
10  void changei (int i);
11  {
12      i = 8;
13  }
```

```
5    1   typedef struct tnode
     2   {
     3      int      x;
     4      double   y;
     5      struct tnode *next;
     6   }NODE;
     7
     8   NODE *lptr1;
     9
    10   if (lptr1 = ((NODE *)
          malloc(sizeof(NODE)))) == NULL)
    11      {
    12      printf ("Out of memory\n");
    13      exit (0);
    14      }


6    1   main ()
     2   {
     3      /* Define a pointer to a function
            with an 'int' as a parameter*/
     4
     5      int *fptr(int len);
     6
     7      *fptr = drawline;
     8
     9      (*fptr) (50);
    10   }
    11
    12   int drawline (int len)
    13   {
    14      while (len > 0)
    15         {
    16         printf ("-");
    17         len--;
    18         }
    19      printf ("\n");
    20   }


7    1   struct node
     2   {
     3      int      x;
     4      double   y;
     5   };
     6
```

```
7    struct node nodearr[50];
8    char *cptr;
9
10   cptr = nodearr;
11   while ((cptr - nodearr) < 50)
12       {
13       cptr->x = 0;
14       cptr->y = 0.0;
15       cptr++;
16       }
```

**8**
```
1    struct node
2    {
3        int     x;
4        double  y;
5    };
6    struct node nodearr[50], *sptr =
                                   nodearr;
7
8    while ((sptr - nodearr)  50)
9        {
10       sptr->x = 0;
11       sptr->y = 0.0;
12       sptr += sizeof(struct node);
13       }
```

# 9   The Standard Libraries

## 9.1   Introduction

It is part of the philosophy of the C programming language that no built-in functions are included in the language definition for such things as: reading and writing files; doing special mathematical functions; performing string manipulation; and doing terminal input/output.

Thus, equivalents to the file READ and WRITE of COBOL, the mathematical functions ABS and SQR of Pascal, and the terminal output sequence PUT SKIP of PL/1 are missing from C.

Functions which provide these 'features' are defined, separately from C's language definition, in a number of standard libraries. The functions are stored in the libraries in their compiled, or object-code, form. They are 'linked' or 'loaded' with the user's program at the load step, after compilation. The output of the load step is an executable program.

Functions, data objects and macros used in the C libraries are declared in standard header files. These should be included in a program which uses C library functions. The standard I/O header file 'stdio.h' is the most important of the standard header files.

Because a large number of standard functions are excluded from the C language definition, the C language itself is small and compilers for it are simpler than for other languages. Only the header files containing references to the functions actually needed are included in a C program; this tends to reduce the size of executable programs.

The programmer is encouraged to use the available functions as 'building blocks' in the construction of complex programs. Any special functions developed by the programmer may become part of the programmer's own library or standard header file and re-used in many programs. A good example of such a function is the 'substr' function shown in Chapter 6.

The full range of header files available to the programmer will be found in the C compiler documentation for the particular environment. A subset of header files and functions that are part of the ANSI C standard is discussed in this chapter.

The header files most commonly used are:

| | |
|---|---|
| 'stdio.h' | standard I-O |
| 'string.h' | string functions |
| 'ctype.h' | character class tests |
| 'math.h' | mathematical functions |
| 'stdlib.h' | other standard functions |

A listing in alphabetic order of the functions declared in these five header files is given in Appendix A.

Other standard header files are:

| | |
|---|---|
| 'assert.h' | diagnostics functions |
| 'time.h' | time and date functions |
| 'stdarg.h' | variable argument functions |
| 'signal.h' | signal/interrupt functions |
| 'setjmp.h' | function control |
| 'limits.h' | implementation limits |
| 'float.h' | magnitude limits |
| 'stddef.h' | common definitions |
| 'errno.h' | errors |
| 'locale.h' | localisation |

## 9.2  Standard I/O

The standard I/O header file 'stdio.h' contains declarations of functions, defined in the C function libraries, which handle transfer of data to and from external devices. 'stdio.h' provides a standard interface to these devices. Using the library functions, the programmer does not have to rely on operating system-dependent I/O procedures.

**Standard I/O files**

'stdio.h' defines three 'standard' files:

| stdin | standard input |
| stdout | standard output |
| stderr | standard error |

All files are connected to 'streams' and the terms 'file' and 'stream' are often used interchangeably. The concept of 'stream' is explained fully in Section 9.4.

- 'stdin' usually means the terminal input device and may be thought of as representing the keyboard.

- 'stdout' usually means the terminal output device and may be thought of as representing the screen.

- Output to 'stderr' is directed to the standard output device, even if 'stdout' is redirected elsewhere, as it may be when using Unix, OS/2 and DOS.

When a C program begins execution, the three standard I/O files are opened automatically and are available to the program from that point.

**Standard I/O functions**

The library function 'getchar' uses standard input to fetch a character of data and assign the data to a variable. 'putchar' similarly uses standard output to write a character to the standard output device.

Two additional functions, 'getc' and 'putc', are supplied in 'stdio.h'. These are more general cases of 'getchar' and 'putchar'.

```
getc(stdin)       is equivalent to  getchar()
putc(c,stdout)    is equivalent to  putchar(c)
```

As shown later in this chapter, 'getc' and 'putc' may be used to do input/output on files other than the standard input and standard output.

'stdio.h' also contains definitions for the symbolic constants NULL (binary zero) and EOF (normally -1).

The file pointer declarator FILE is defined in 'stdio.h', as is the size, BUFSIZ, of the underlying file I/O buffer.

'stdio.h' provides functions for formatted console input/output. We have already seen 'printf', which is used for output to the standard output device. Up to now, for string input, we have used the function 'gets'; the input counterpart of 'printf', which performs similar functions to 'gets', is 'scanf'.

Here is a list of useful 'stdio.h' functions and definitions:

| | |
|---|---|
| stdin | Standard input |
| stdout | Standard output |
| stderr | Standard error |
| EOF | End of file |
| NULL | Null character |
| FILE | File pointer declarator |
| BUFSIZ | File I/O buffer size |
| getc(fp) | Return a character from file pointed to by fp |
| getchar() | Return a character from standard input |
| putc(c,fp) | Put character c on file pointed to by fp |
| putchar(c) | Put character c to the standard output |
| gets(s) | Read text from standard input until newline, copy to string s and null-terminate |
| puts(s) | Write string s and a newline to the standard output |
| fopen(s,m) | Open file named in string s in access mode m |
| fclose(fp) | Close file pointed to by fp |

| | |
|---|---|
| `fgets(s,n,fp)` | Read from file pointed to by `fp`, maximum `n` characters into string `s` |
| `fputs(s, fp)` | Write string `s` to file pointed to by `fp` |
| `fread(s,sz,ct,fp)` | |
| | Buffered read from file pointed to by `fp` of `ct` objects of size `sz` into the buffer `s` |
| `fwrite(s,sz,ct,fp)` | |
| | Buffered write to file pointed to by `fp` of `ct` objects of size `sz` from the buffer `s` |
| `fflush(fp)` | Flush a file buffer |
| `fseek(fp,n,o)` | Set file pointer `n` bytes from `o`, 'origin', which is defined as a set of macros in 'stdio.h' |
| `printf(f,args)` | Write the values represented by `args` to standard output according to the format codes specified in the format string `f` |
| `scanf(f,args)` | Read from standard input the values represented by `args` according to the format codes specified in the format string `f` |
| `fprintf(fp,f,args)` | |
| | Write to a file pointed to by `fp` the values represented by `args` according to the format codes specified in the format string `f` |
| `fscanf(fp,f,args)` | |
| | Read from a file pointed to by `fp` the values represented by `args` according to the format codes specified in the format string `f` |

```
sprintf(s,f,args)
```

> Same as 'printf' except that the output is written to the string s

```
sscanf(s,f,args)
```

> Same as 'scanf' except that the input is taken from the string s

'fp' is an arbitrary name which here denotes 'file pointer'. The file pointer is of type 'FILE *'. 'FILE' is defined in 'stdio.h' as a structure type, using 'typedef'.

The structure pointed to by the file pointer holds all information necessary to control file access, including a pointer which keeps track of the read/write position in the file.

The file pointer is used to access a file by all the file open, close, read and write functions. 'stdin', 'stdout' and 'stderr' are examples of special file pointers.

Details of all functions declared in 'stdio.h' can be found in Appendix A.

## 9.3 Printf and Scanf

The formatted output and input functions, 'printf' and 'scanf', are declared in 'stdio.h'; they are so heavily used and have so many syntax options that they deserve to be treated separately.

Here are their function prototypes:

```
int printf (const char *<format>,
            <varlist>);
int scanf  (const char *<format>,
            <varlist>);
```

There is also a number of variants of both functions: 'fprintf' for formatted output to file; 'sprintf' for formatted output to strings; 'fscanf' and 'sscanf' for formatted input from files and strings.

Up to now, in place of 'scanf', we have used the function 'gets' to read text from the standard input. 'scanf' and 'printf' are big, powerful functions with many options. For simple text input, 'gets' may be more efficient than 'scanf'. Equally, for simple text output, 'puts' may be more efficient than 'printf'. Often, however, the additional capabilities of 'printf' and 'scanf' are needed.

### Printf

The 'printf' function in general has two sets of arguments: the format string and a variable list. The format string contains ordinary characters, which are copied to the standard output and, optionally, format codes, which are letters prefixed by a '%'. For each format code specified in the format string, there must be a corresponding variable in the variable list which is of the data type implied by the format code.

'printf' returns an integer value which represents the number of characters output.

Here is a list of the 'printf' format codes and their meanings:

| | |
|---|---|
| d,i,o,u, x, X | The variable corresponding to the format code is converted to decimal (d,i), octal (o), unsigned decimal (u) or unsigned hexadecimal (x and X). The x conversion uses the letters abcdef; X uses ABCDEF. |
| | The format string can specify a minimum width for any field by specifying a decimal number after the '%'. |
| f | The variable is converted to a decimal notation of form [-]ddd.ddd, where the minimum width (w) of the field and the precision (p) are specified by %w.pf. If no width or precision specification is given, the default precision is 6 characters; a precision |

| | |
|---|---|
| | of zero causes the decimal point to be suppressed. |
| e,E | The float or double variable is converted to 'scientific notation' of form [-]d.ddde±dd. Width and precision may also be specified. The default precision is 6 characters; a precision of zero causes the decimal point to be suppressed. |
| g,G | The float or double variable is printed in style f or e. Style e is used only if the exponent resulting from the conversion is less than -4 or greater than the precision. Trailing zeroes are removed. A decimal point appears only if it is followed by a digit. |
| c | The variable is printed as a character. |
| s | The variable is taken to be a string (character pointer) and characters from the string are printed until a null character is encountered or the number of characters indicated by the precision specification is reached. |
| p | Print variable as a pointer of type 'void *'. |
| n | The associated variable is a pointer to an integer which is assigned the number of characters written so far by 'printf' on this call. |
| % | Print a '%'. |

Using these format codes, very sophisticated output is possible using 'printf'.

Here is a simple example program which uses 'printf' to print a table of squares and cubes of the numbers from 1 to 19:

```
#include "stdio.h"

main()
{
    float f;

    for (f=1.0; f < 20.0;  f++)
        printf ("%6.2f %6.2f %6.2f\n", f,
                f*f,  f*f*f);
}
```

In this case, the format code '%6.2f' causes the corresponding floating-point number to be printed so that they occupy at least six spaces of width, including two digits after the decimal point.

**Scanf**

The format codes used by 'scanf' and all variants of both 'printf' and 'scanf' are superficially similar. The are, however, some important differences:

● 'scanf' allows specification of field width but not of precision; the field width is a maximum, while for 'printf' it is a minimum value

● The '[]' conversion sequence is peculiar to 'scanf'.

● 'scanf' does not accept 'printf' flag characters (see Appendix A).

Therefore, despite the similarity, the format codes for 'printf' should not be used as a guide to those of 'scanf', or vice-versa.

Here is a list of the 'scanf' format codes:

d,i,o,u,x    Read a decimal, integer, octal, unsigned or hexadecimal number from standard input and place at an integer pointer specified in the argument list.

e,f,g        Read a floating-point number and place at a 'float' pointer specified in the argument list.

| c,s | Read: (c) a number of characters (default 1); (s) a string. In both cases place the input at a character pointer specified in the argument list. |
| --- | --- |
| p | Read a pointer (of type 'void *', as output by 'printf') and place at a pointer specified in the argument list. |
| n | Assign to the associated argument (int *) the number of characters so far read by this call. |
| [] | Read the longest string of input characters from the scan set between brackets and place at a character pointer specified in the argument list. A null terminator is added. |
| [^] | Read the longest set of input characters not from the scan set between brackets and place at a character pointer specified in the argument list. A null terminator is added. |
| % | Literal '%'; no assignment. |

'scanf' is the input form of 'printf'. Like 'printf', it uses two sets of arguments: a format string and a variable list. The 'scanf' function reads from the standard input one or more data objects, performs appropriate conversions on them according to the format string specification, and stores the results at the pointers which are specified in the variable list.

Each variable in the variable list must be a pointer. The pointer type should be the same as the type of data object implied by the corresponding format code.

With 'scanf', it is not possible to display a prompt as part of the format string. If a prompt is required, the 'scanf' call should be preceded by a 'printf'.

A non-whitespace character in the 'scanf' format string causes 'scanf' to read and discard a matching input character. For example:

```
scanf ("%d/%d/%d", &dd, &mm, &yy);
```

This works when slashes are entered as part of the date input.

'scanf' stops reading from standard input when it exhausts its format string or encounters a mismatch between one of its format codes and an input data item. It returns as its value the number of data objects read and successfully converted, or EOF if end-of-file or error occurs before any input conversion.

If there is more input data than is required by an item in the 'scanf' variable list, unused data will be used by 'scanf' as input to the next item, if any.

As an example use of 'scanf', the 'get_data' function in the program 'dates.c' could have been written more simply like this:

```
int get_data ()
{
    printf ("Enter the day number ");
    scanf ("%d", &idd);
    printf ("Enter the month number ");
    scanf ("%d", &imm);
    printf ("Enter the year number ");
    scanf ("%d", &iyy);
}
```

Input of characters to an array using library functions such as 'gets', followed by explicit conversion calls to 'atoi' and 'atof' are replaced by the functionality of 'scanf'.

### Sprintf and other functions
The function 'sprintf' is the same as 'printf' except that, instead of writing to standard output, it places the output at a memory address specified by a character pointer and terminates the output with a null character.

The character pointer must be initialised to the address of a character array big enough to take the output of the 'sprintf' conversion.

The program above, which uses 'printf' to print a table of squares and cubes, could be implemented with 'sprintf':

```
#include "stdio.h"

main ()
{
    float f;
    char outstr[100];

    for (f=1.0; f < 20.0; f++)
        {
        sprintf (outstr, "%6.2f %6.2f
                %6.2f\n", f, f*f, f*f*f);
        printf ("%s",outstr);
        }
}
```

'sscanf' is the same as 'scanf' except that it takes its input from a string rather than from standard input.

'fprintf' and 'fscanf' are the file versions of 'printf' and 'scanf'; they write to and read from files according to rules which are described in the next section.

## 9.4   File handling

The concept of a file in C has its genesis in the original definition of a file in the Unix operating system. A file is an unstructured collection of character data. A file may represent a disk file or any peripheral device.

C assumes that the file has no structure: there is no concept inherent in the language of file records, block sizes or similar structures. Any file structure must be imposed on the raw file by the program logic itself.

A *stream* is the conceptual source or destination of data associated with a physical file. A stream is a consistent interface to the C programmer which is independent of the actual device being accessed. An 'open' operation, such as 'fopen', associates a stream with a file by means of the file pointer. Once a file is open, information may be exchanged between it and a C program.

The 'stdio.h' file-access functions, given in Section 9.2 above, operate on files via streams. A stream may be thought of as a data object of type:

```
FILE *
```

or 'file pointer'. Each file has a pointer which records the 'current position' in the file. The pointer is used to open and close the file, to read from and write to it and to perform 'random access' using the 'fseek' library function.

These are the function prototypes, which are included in 'stdio.h', for 'fopen' and 'fclose':

```
FILE *fopen (const char *s, const char
        *mode);

int fclose (FILE *fp);
```

### Example – copying a file
Figure 9.1 includes a simple program which copies one disk file to another.

First, two file pointers are defined: inp and outp.

The two character arrays are initialised to the names of the input and output files from data input by the user. The familiar 'gets' function is used to initialise these strings.

Next, the program attempts to open both files, the first in read mode ("r") and the second in write mode ("w"). 'fopen' returns an object of type 'FILE *' which is used subsequently to access the file opened. If either file cannot be opened, the program terminates abnormally.

If the file in read mode cannot be opened, it probably means that the input file is not there to be copied. If the write mode file cannot be opened, it is created. It is unlikely that the program would end abnormally as a result of inability to open a file for output.

```c
/*
Program filecopy.c
*/

#include "stdio.h"
#include "stdlib.h"

void filecopy (FILE *, FILE *);

main()
{
    /* Define input and output file
       pointers */

    FILE *inp, *outp;
    char  inname[20], outname[20];

    printf ("Enter input file name ");
    gets (inname);
    printf ("Enter output file name ");
    gets (outname);

    if ((inp = fopen(inname, "r")) ==
             NULL)
       {
       printf ("Cannot open input file\n");
       exit (0);
       }
    if ((outp = fopen(outname, "w")) ==
             NULL)
       {
       printf ("Cannot open output file\n");
       exit (0);
       }

    filecopy (inp, outp);

    fclose (inp);
    fclose (outp);
}

void filecopy (FILE *inp, FILE *outp)
{
    int c;

    while ((c = getc(inp)) != EOF)
        putc (c, outp);
}
```

*Figure 9.1*

The function 'filecopy' is called with the file pointers inp and outp as parameters. 'filecopy' uses the 'stdio.h' functions 'getc' and 'putc' to read from the input file, one character at a time, and write to the output file. The reads stop when EOF on the input file is encountered.

Finally, in 'main', the two file pointers are supplied as parameters to the 'fclose' library function, which closes the files, disassociates the files from the streams and frees the file pointers.

All the library functions used in 'filecopy.c' in turn call low-level system-specific functions which do the file operations at a lower level. The 'stdio.h' functions ensure a high-level, system-independent interface to files on any system.

It may seem surprising that 'getc' and 'putc' are used to read and write data on a character-by-character basis. More powerful functions, such as 'fgets' and 'fputs' both perform repeated calls on 'getc' and 'putc'.

### Access modes

The legal access modes for use with the 'fopen' function on text files are these:

"r"      Open a text file for reading and position the read/write pointer at the beginning of the file.

"w"      Open a text file for writing; if it does not already exist, create it; if it does exist, delete it.

"a"      Append to a text file; position the read/write pointer at the end of the file; if the file does not already exist, create it.

"r+"     Open a text file for reading and writing; otherwise same as "r".

"w+"     Open a text file for reading and writing; otherwise same as "w".

"a+"     Append to a text file for reading and writing; otherwise same as "a".

If an access mode is suffixed with 'b' in the manner "wb" or "a+b", a binary stream is specified.

### Text and binary files

The ANSI standard specifies text and binary streams. On some systems, especially Unix, there is no difference at all between the two.

A text stream is a sequence of lines, terminated by '\n' and containing zero or more characters, which may undergo certain character translations by the local environment.

A binary stream undergoes no such translations and, on a given system, will always read the same as it was written.

Where binary streams are distinguished from text streams, the behaviour of some standard library functions is altered.

### Fgets and Fputs

The 'fgets' and 'fputs' functions provide a higher-level means of reading from and writing to files than 'getc' and 'putc'.

'fgets' and 'fputs' have the following function prototypes:

```
char  *fgets(char *s, int n, FILE *fp);

int   fputs(const char *s, FILE *fp);
```

These prototypes are in 'stdio.h'.

The 'fgets' function reads a string from a specified file until either a newline character or a number of characters one less than s have been read. The resulting string is null-terminated. Any newline character read is included in the string.

The 'fputs' function writes to the output file a null-terminated string pointed to by s, followed by a newline character. The null character is not copied.

### Example – searching a file

Figure 9.2 is a more complex example of a file-processing program using most of the file access functions we have seen so far. The program reads a file line-by-line and searches each line for an occurrence of a specified pattern of characters. The total number of occurrences in the file, if any, is reported.

```
/*
    fsearch.c
*/
#include "stdio.h"
#include "stdlib.h"
#include "string.h"

main()
{
    char filename[20], pattern[100];
    char instr[100], *cp1, *cp2;
    int  matchct, pos, inlen;
    FILE *inp;

    printf ("Enter file name ");
    gets (filename);
    printf ("Enter pattern to be found ");
    gets (pattern);

    if ((inp = fopen(filename, "r")) ==
                NULL)
        {
        printf ("Cannot open input file\n");
        exit (0);
        }

    matchct = 0;
    cp2 = pattern;

    while ((fgets(instr, 100, inp)) != NULL)
        {
        /* search each line until end file */

        cp1 = instr;
        inlen = strlen(cp2);
        while ((pos=strpos(cp1, cp2)) >= 0)
            {
            matchct++;
            cp1 += (pos + inlen - 1);
            }
        }
    printf ("%d occurrences of %s in file %s\n",
            matchct, pattern,
            filename);
    fclose (inp);
}
```

*Figure 9.2*

This program uses the function 'strpos', borrowed from Figure 6.5, to search in each line returned from the file by 'fgets' for the pattern required.

The arrays holding the file name and pattern are initialised after input of user data by 'gets'.

'fgets' reads a line of the file into the array instr. Two local character pointers are set to the addresses of instr and pattern respectively. If a match is found in a given line, the pointer to instr is incremented to allow a possible second match in that line to be found.

Finally, the number of matches is reported and the file closed.

No attempt is made to find a pattern match spanning the end of one line and the beginning of the next. This is a tricky problem; think about it.

A program such as this might form the basis for pattern matching and search/replace functions in a screen editor.

**Buffered file access**

Lastly, let us consider some library functions which are used for formatted and 'buffered' file access. They are more general than 'fgets' and 'fputs', and they allow more sophisticated operations on files.

Prototypes of the functions follow:

```
int fscanf (FILE *fp, const char
     *<format>, <variable list>);

int fprintf (FILE *fp, const char
     *<format>, <variable list>);

unsigned fread (void *buf, unsigned n,
     unsigned count, FILE *fp);

unsigned fwrite (void *buf, unsigned n,
     unsigned count, FILE *fp);

int fseek (FILE *fp, long n, int origin);

int fflush (FILE *fp);

int feof (FILE *fp);

int ferror (FILE *fp);
```

'fscanf' and 'fprintf' are used in exactly the same way as 'scanf' and 'printf', with exactly the same parameters, except that they access files and have an additional argument which is a file pointer. They perform I/O character-by-character with the underlying standard I/O file buffer; the characters are formatted according to the format codes specified. Because of the provision for formatting, they may be slower than 'fread' and 'fwrite'.

The 'fread' and 'fwrite' functions are used for 'buffered' or 'direct' I/O. The 'stdio.h' file I/O functions we have used up to now do character-by-character I/O with the file buffer. 'fread' reads a block of data from the standard I/O file buffer. 'fwrite' writes a block of data to the buffer. For large volumes of data, this type of buffered I/O is faster than the character-based equivalent.

Where the distinction between text and binary streams is implemented, 'fread' and 'fwrite' may be used with either, but are usually used with binary streams.

For 'fread', buf is a pointer to a region of memory that will receive the data read from the file. For 'fwrite', buf is a pointer to the information that is to be written to the file.

The number of bytes to be read or written is specified by n. The argument count determines how many items of n bytes long will be read or written. fp in both cases is the file pointer.

'fread' returns an integer value representing the number of objects read. Exception conditions following an 'fread' call are checked with the functions 'ferror' and 'feof'.

'ferror' checks whether a file operation has produced an error, in which case it returns a non-zero value. Similarly, 'feof' returns a non-zero value if an end-of-file condition is encountered.

'fwrite' returns an integer value representing the number of objects written, or a number less than count if there is an error.

'fseek' is used to implement a form of 'random access'. For binary streams (binary and text streams, if no distinction is implemented) the function causes the file pointer to be set to a displacement of n characters from origin.

'fflush' causes the contents of any buffered but unwritten data to be written to the file pointed to by fp.

### Example – creating a record-based file

The program in Figure 9.3, called 'bufio.c', uses buffered I/O functions to create a file of 'records' from data input by the user; it then dumps to standard output the contents of the file, starting at a point selected by the user.

```
/* Program 'bufio.c', creates a file called
   'file.dat' using 'fwrite' from user input and
   dumps the file to standard output starting at
   an offset specified by the user        */

#include "stdio.h"
#include "stdlib.h"
#define NOT_OK 1
#define OK 0

struct file_rec
    {
    char     fname[15];
    char     lname[15];
    char     city[20];
    char     soc_sec_no[8];
    int      age;
    int      height_cm;
    char     sex;
    };

/* Function prototype declarations */

int f_create (void);
int f_dump (long);
void p_stdout (struct file_rec *);

main()
{
    int c;
    int start_rec = 0;
    long start_off = 0;

    if ((f_create()) == NOT_OK)
        {
        printf ("Couldn't create output file\n");
        exit (0);
        }
```

```c
    fflush (stdin);
    printf ("\nThe file will now be printed\n");
    printf ("Print from the start? Answer 'y' or
             'n' and RETURN: ");
    if ((c = getchar ()) == 'n')
        {
        fflush (stdin);
        printf ("Start with what record no.? Enter
                                    and RETURN: ");
        scanf ("%d", &start_rec);

        /* Subtract one to get offset intended */

        start_rec--;
        if (start_rec < 0)
            start_rec = 0;
        start_off = (long) start_rec *
                ((long) sizeof (struct file_rec));
        }

    if ((f_dump (start_off)) == NOT_OK)
        {
        printf ("Couldn't print file just
                                    created\n");
        exit (0);
        }
}

int f_create (void)
{
    struct file_rec buf;
    FILE *outp;
    int c;

    /* Create output file */

    if ((outp = fopen ("file.dat","wb")) == NULL)
        {
        printf ("Couldn't open output file\n");
        return (NOT_OK);
        }

    do
        {
        /* Enter one record of data */

        printf ("Enter first name and last name: ");
        scanf ("%s %s", buf.fname, buf.lname);
        printf ("Enter city: ");
        scanf ("%s", buf.city);
        printf ("Enter social security number: ");
        scanf ("%s", buf.soc_sec_no);
        printf ("Enter age, height in cm., sex
                                    (M or F): ");
        scanf ("%d %d %c", &buf.age,
                &buf.height_cm, &buf.sex);
```

```
        /* Flush standard input to get rid of any
           unwanted 'scanf' stuff */

        fflush (stdin);

        /* Write the record to the file */

        if ((fwrite (&buf, sizeof(buf), 1, outp)) < 1)
            {
            printf ("Couldn't write to output
                                        file\n");
            return (NOT_OK);
            }

        printf ("Press RETURN to enter more data,
                                 'q' to quit: ");
        }
    while ((c = getchar()) != 'q');

    fclose (outp);
    return (OK);
}

int f_dump (long start_off)
{
    struct file_rec buf;
    FILE *inp;
    int end_of_file = 0;

    if ((inp = fopen ("file.dat","rb")) == NULL)
        {
        printf ("Can't open file which has just
                                been created\n");
        return (NOT_OK);
        }

    if (start_off > 0)
        if ((fseek (inp, start_off, SEEK_SET)) != 0)
            {
            printf ("Can't get to file offset
                                    requested\n");
            return (NOT_OK);
            }

    while (end_of_file == 0)
        {
        fread (&buf, sizeof(buf), 1, inp);
        if ((ferror (inp)) != 0)
            {
            printf ("Error reading file\n");
            return (NOT_OK);
            }
        if ((feof (inp)) != 0)
            {
            printf ("End of file reached\n");
            end_of_file = 1;
            }
        else
```

```
            p_stdout (&buf);
        }
    fclose (inp);
    return (OK);
}

void p_stdout (struct file_rec *buf)

{
    printf ("\nName: %s %s\n", buf->fname,
            buf->lname);
    printf ("City: %s\n", buf->city);
    printf ("Social security number: %s\n",
            buf->soc_sec_no);
    printf ("Age, height, sex: %d %d %c\n",
            buf->age, buf->height_cm, buf->sex);
    printf ("\n");
}
```

*Figure 9.3*

The 'main' function of 'bufio.c' carries out three tasks: create the file 'file.dat'; accept user input, defining the point in the file from which data will be output; and dump the required portion of the file to standard output.

The function 'fcreate' is called to create the file 'file.dat' and to initialise it with data input by the user. The file is set up as a sequence of 'records' defined by the structure type 'struct file_rec'.

Remember that C has no concept of 'file record' as an inherent part of a file; here the conceptual 'record' is an arbitrary data structure, 'struct file_rec', defined by the programmer.

In 'f_create', the file is opened as a binary stream in write mode. The formatted input function 'scanf' is repeatedly called and accepts user-input data, which is stored in the structure buf and which is then used as a 'record' to write to the file using the 'fwrite' function. The whole sequence is repeated until directed otherwise by the user.

The 'fflush' function call after the 'scanf' statements is used to ensure that any data left over after user input is cleared from the standard input buffer. If this were not done, it is possible that left-over data would be used by 'getchar' in the loop-control condition, with unintended results.

'fwrite', on error, returns an integral value less than the count of items to be written, in this case 1. 'fwrite' uses the address of the structure 'buf' as its output buffer area. The size of the buffer to be written is found using the 'sizeof' operator.

Finally, when all data has been written to the file, 'file.dat' is closed with 'fclose'.

On return to 'main' from 'fwrite', the user is asked to indicate the point in the file, or 'record' number, from which output is to be started. This number is accepted from the standard input using 'scanf'.

The 'record' number input by the user is multiplied by the size of the 'record' to produce the required start offset in bytes. Note that the 'record' number is first decremented by one to take account of the fact that the first 'record' has a zero offset.

The resulting byte offset is used as a parameter by 'f_dump'. In 'f_dump', if the value of the byte offset is greater than zero, 'fseek' is called to move the file pointer from the start of the file to the byte offset defined by start_off.

The macro values SEEK_SET (file start), SEEK_CUR (current position) and SEEK_END (end of file) are defined in 'stdio.h'.

Next, 'fread' is repeatedly called to read into its buffer buf 'records' previously written. The function 'p_stdout' is used on each iteration to dump the contents of buf to the standard output.

Any error condition resulting from 'fread' is tested for, using 'ferror'; 'feof' otherwise reports end-of-file. When end-of-file is reached, the file is closed, control returned to 'main' and the program stops.

Using similar data structures and standard I/O functions to those used in 'bufio.c', advanced file handling and retrieval systems may be built using C which are largely independent of the host operating system and environment.

## 9.5 String functions

Declarations of standard string-manipulation functions available to the programmer are found in the string header file 'string.h'.

The most common of these functions were given in Section 6.5; here is a fuller list.

---

```
char *strcat (char *s1, const char *s2)
```

The function 'strcat' appends a copy of string s2 to the end of s1 and returns a pointer to the null-terminated result.

---

```
char *strncat (char *s1, const char
              *s2, int n)
```

'strncat' appends at most n characters from s2 to s1 and returns a pointer to the null-terminated result.

---

```
int strcmp (const char *s1, const char
                  *s2)
```

'strcmp' compares its arguments and returns an integer less than, equal to or greater than zero according to whether s1 is lexicographically less than, equal to or greater than s2.

---

```
int strncmp (const char *s1, const char
                  *s2, int n)
```

'strncmp' is the same as 'strcmp', but compares at most n characters.

---

```
char *strcpy(char *s1, const char *s2)
```

'strcpy' copies string s2 to s1, stopping after the null character has been copied and returning a pointer to s1.

```
char *strncpy (char *s1, const char
              s2, int n)
```

'strncpy' copies exactly n characters, truncating s2 or adding null characters to s1 if necessary. The result is not null-terminated if the length of s2 is n or more. A pointer to s1 is returned.

---

```
int strlen (const char *s)
```

'strlen' returns the number of characters in s, not counting the null-terminator.

---

```
char *strchr (const char *s, int c)
```

'strchr' returns a pointer to the first occurrence of character c in string s or a NULL pointer if c does not occur in s.

---

```
char *strrchr (const char *s, int c)
```

'strrchr' is the same as 'strchr' except that a pointer to the last occurrence of the character in the string is returned.

---

```
char *strpbrk (const char *s1, const
              char *s2)
```

'strpbrk' returns a pointer to the first occurrence in string s1 of any character from string s2, or a NULL character if there is no match.

---

```
int strspn (const char *s1, const char
            *s2)
```

'strspn' returns the length of the initial segment of s1 which consists entirely of characters from s2.

---

## 9.6   Character class tests

The standard header file 'ctype.h' provides a set of useful functions which perform tests on single-character data in a way that is not system-dependent.

Suppose that, on a system which uses the ASCII character set, the following test is made:

```
char c;
   .
   .
/* initialise  c  here  */
   .
   .
if ((c >= 'a') && (c <= 'z'))
    printf ("Lower-case alphabetic\n");
```

The test will be successful and the message printed when it should be. If the system uses the EBCDIC character set however, the test will not work because the characters from a to z in EBCDIC are not numerically contiguous.

All the functions in 'ctype.h' provide a programming interface which is independent of such problems.

All of the functions return a non-zero integer value representing TRUE, and a zero value for FALSE. They all take one argument of type 'int', which is treated as a character.

The following is a list of the functions:

| | |
|---|---|
| int isalpha (int c) | alphabetic: a-z, A-Z |
| int isupper (int c) | upper case: A-Z |
| int islower (int c) | lower case: a-z |
| int isdigit (int c) | digit: 0-9 |
| int isxdigit (int c) | hexadecimal digit: 0-9, a-f, A-F |
| int isalnum (int c) | alphabetic or digit |
| int isspace (int c) | blank |

```
int ispunct (int c)          not alphanumeric or
                             control or space

int isprint (int c)          any printable character

int isgraph (int c)          like 'isprint', except
                             false for space

int iscntrl (int c)          control character,
                             including DEL
```

## 9.7  Mathematical functions

The 'math.h' standard header file provides a set of mathematical functions and macros which all take 'double' arguments and return 'double' values.

The 'math.h' header also defines a macro called 'HUGE_VAL'. If an operation produces a result which is too large to be represented by a 'double', 'HUGE_VAL' is returned; this denotes a range error.

The functions provided are classified as trigonometric, hyperbolic, exponential/logarithmic and miscellaneous.

### Trigonometric functions
The following are the trigonometric functions.

```
double sin (double x)
```

Returns sine of x in radians.

```
double cos (double x)
```

Returns cosine of x in radians.

```
double tan (double x)
```

Returns tangent of x in radians.

```
double asin (double x)
```

Returns arcsine of x in the range -PI/2 to PI/2.

```
double acos (double x)
```

Returns arccosine of x in the range zero to PI.

---

```
double atan (double x)
```

Returns the arctangent of x in the range -PI/2 to PI/2.

---

```
double atan2 (double y, double x)
```

Returns the arctangent of y/x in the range -PI to PI using the signs of both arguments to determine the quadrant of the return value.

---

**Hyperbolic functions**
These are the hyperbolic functions:

---

```
double sinh (double x)
```

Returns the hyperbolic sine of x.

---

```
double cosh (double x)
```

Returns the hyperbolic cosine of x.

---

```
double tanh (double x)
```

Returns the hyperbolic tangent of x.

---

**Logarithmic and exponential functions**
Here are the logarithmic and exponential functions:

---

```
double exp (double x)
```

Returns the value of 'e' raised to the power of x.

---

```
double log (double x)
```

Returns the natural logarithm of x.

```
double log10 (double x)
```

Returns the logarithm to base 10 of x.

```
double pow (double x, double y)
```

Returns the value of x raised to the power y.

```
double sqrt (double x)
```

Returns the non-negative square root of x; the value of x must not be negative.

**Miscellaneous functions**
Finally, the miscellaneous functions:

```
double floor (double x)
```

Returns the largest integer not greater than x.

```
double ceil (double x)
```

Returns the smallest integer not less than x.

```
double fabs (double x)
```

Returns the absolute value of x: $|x|$.

```
double fmod (double x, double y)
```

Returns the remainder of the division of x by y.

## 9.8 Other functions

Here is a list of useful utility functions declared in the header file 'stdlib.h'. The type 'size_t' is defined, using 'typedef' in 'stddef.h' as an 'unsigned int'.

---

```
int atoi (const char *s)
```

Converts the string s to 'int'.

---

```
double atof (const char *s)
```

Converts the string s to a double floating-point number.

---

```
long atol (const char *s)
```

Converts the string s to a long integer.

---

```
void *malloc (size_t size)
```

Allocates in memory the amount of space needed to accommodate 'size' and returns a pointer to that memory.

---

```
void free (void *p)
```

Frees the memory pointed to by p.

---

```
void *calloc (size_t n, size_t size)
```

Returns a pointer to memory space for an array of n objects of size size.

---

```
void *realloc (void *p, size_t size)
```

Changes the size of the object pointed to by p to size.

---

```
void exit (int status)
```

Causes program termination. The status returned is handled in a system-dependent way; zero is interpreted as successful termination.

```
int abs (int n)
```

Returns the absolute value of n.

---

## Find the error

In each of the programs below, identify the line containing the error. Answers are given in Appendix C.

```
1    1   #include "stdio.h"
     2   void filecopy (FILE *, FILE *);
     3   main()
     4   {
     5      FILE *inp, *outp;
     6      char inname[20], outname[20];
     7
     8      printf ("Enter input file name: ");
     9      gets (inname);
    10      printf ("Enter output file name: ");
    11      gets (outname);
    12
    13      if ((inp = fopen(inname, "r")) == NULL)
    14         {
    15         printf ("Cannot open input
                                      file\n");
    16         exit (0);
    17         }
    18
    19      if ((outp = fopen(outname, "r")) == NULL
    20         {
    21         printf ("Cannot open output
                                      file\n");
    22         exit (0);
    23         }
    24
    25      filecopy (inp, outp);
    26
    27      fclose (inp);
    28      fclose (outp);
    29   }
    30
    31   void filecopy (FILE *inp, FILE *outp)
    32   {
```

```
33      int c;
34
35      while ((c = getc(inp)) != EOF)
36          putc (c, outp);
37  }
```

```
2   1   #include "stdio.h"
    2   void filecopy (FILE *, FILE *);
    3   main()
    4   {
    5       FILE *inp, *outp;
    6       char inname[20], outname[20];
    7
    8       printf ("Enter input file name: ");
    9       gets (inname);
    10      printf ("Enter output file name: ");
    11      gets (outname);
    12
    13      if ((inp = fopen(inname, "r")) == NULL)
    14          {
    15          printf ("Cannot open input
                                    file\n");
    16          exit (0);
    17          }
    18
    19      if ((outp = fopen(outname, "w")) == NULL)
    20          {
    21          printf ("Cannot open output
                                    file\n");
    22          exit (0);
    23          }
    24
    25      filecopy (inp, outp);
    26  }
    27
    28  void filecopy (FILE *inp, FILE *outp)
    29  {
    30      int c;
    31
    32      while ((c = getc(inp)) != EOF)
    33          putc (c, outp);
    34  }
```

**3**

```
 1  #include "stdio.h"
 2  void filecopy (FILE *, FILE *);
 3  main()
 4  {
 5      FILE *inp, *outp;
 6      char inname[20], outname[20];
 7
 8      printf ("Enter input file name ");
 9      scanf ("%s",&inname);
10      printf ("Enter output file name ");
11      scanf ("%s",&outname);
12
13      if ((inp = fopen(inname, "r")) == NULL)
14          {
15          printf ("Cannot open input
                                  file\n");
16          exit (0);
17          }
18
19      if ((outp = fopen(outname, "w")) == NULL)
20          {
21          printf ("Cannot open output
                                  file\n");
22          exit (0);
23          }
24
25      filecopy (inp, outp);
26
27      fclose (inp);
28      fclose (outp);
29  }
30
31  void filecopy (FILE *inp, FILE *outp)
32  {
33      int c;
34
35      while ((c = getc(inp)) != EOF)
36          putc (c, outp);
37  }
```

# 10 Other C Features

## 10.1 Command-line arguments

In all examples presented in earlier chapters, data has always been entered to the programs by means of user input via such functions as 'gets' and 'scanf'. The 'main' function has never been supplied with arguments.

It is possible for the 'main' function to take parameters so that the user can enter a command at the shell level of the operating system. In the example of the program 'filecopy.c' from Chapter 9, this would be something like this:

```
filecopy file1 file2
```

The file names are entered on the command line instead of having to be input in response to a prompt when the program is executing.

The command line arguments 'argc' and 'argv' are used as the arguments of 'main' for this purpose.

The 'main' function header with command-line arguments looks like this:

```
main (int argc, char *argv[])
```

argc is an integer value which holds the number of arguments on the command line. Its minimum value is 1, because the name of the program qualifies as an argument. In the 'filecopy' example above, the value of argc is 3.

argv is a pointer to an array of character pointers. Each of the character pointers in the array points to a string. Each of the strings is a single command line argument. Again considering the 'filecopy' example:

```
argv[0]     points to    "filecopy"
argv[1]     points to    "file1"
argv[2]     points to    "file2"
```

The empty brackets '[]' of argv indicate that it is an array of undetermined length. Its actual length is established at run-time, when it is initialised with the command-line arguments entered by the user.

Figure 10.1 shows the program 'filecopy.c' reworked to take command-line arguments.

The 'main' header could also be written:

```
main (int argc, char **argv)
```

```
#include "stdio.h"
#include "stdlib.h"

void filecopy (FILE *, FILE *);

main (int argc, char *argv[])
{
    FILE *inp, *outp;

    if (argc != 3)
        {
        printf ("Invalid parameters\n");
        exit (0);
        }
    if ((inp = fopen(argv[1], "r")) == NULL)
        {
        printf ("Cannot open input file\n");
        exit (0);
        }
    if ((outp = fopen(argv[2], "w")) ==
            NULL)
        {
        printf ("Cannot open output file\n");
        exit (0);
        }

    filecopy (inp, outp);

    fclose (inp);
    fclose (outp);
}

void filecopy (FILE *inp, FILE *outp)
{
    int c;

    while ((c = getc(inp)) != EOF)
        putc (c, outp);
}
```

*Figure 10.1*

`*argv` could be used in place of `argv[0]`, `*++argv` in place of `argv[1]` and then `*++argv` instead of `argv[2]`.

In this case, the need to keep track of pointers is less convenient than using subscripts. Any performance overhead caused by subscripting a three-element array is negligible, which is why double indirection on command-line arguments is often not used.

## 10.2 The C preprocessor

We have already seen some of the C preprocessor directives and have used them to '#define' symbolic constants and to '#include' header files.

The C preprocessor carries out a pass on the program source code before the compiler and interprets all lines having the hash character '#' as the first non-whitespace character.

The '#define' directive causes a name to become defined as a macro to the preprocessor. A macro is a shorthand name for a sequence of tokens which follow. The term 'macro' includes 'symbolic constant'.

Macro names (also called simply 'names') throughout the program are substituted with the value associated with them by the '#define' directive. Header files that are included in the program (with '#include') are expanded and their full source code is substituted in the program for compilation.

Here are the valid C preprocessor directives:

```
#define
#include

#if
#endif
#ifdef
#ifndef
#else
#elif
#undef
```

```
#line

#error
#pragma

#
```

The first two directives are used all the time; the next seven are mainly used for conditional compilation and debugging purposes. The following three give the programmer control over the compilation process and are less often used than the others. '#error' and '#pragma' are new with ANSI C.

'#' is the 'null directive'.

### #ifdef and #ifndef

The '#ifdef' and '#ifndef' directives are often used for debugging purposes and for conditional compilation. The form of both is as follows:

```
#if(n)def <macro name>
    <statement sequence>
#endif
```

If, using '#ifdef', the macro name has been previously defined in a '#define' directive, the statement sequence is compiled. Using '#ifndef', if the macro name has not been previously defined, the statement sequence is compiled. Here is a simple illustrative example:

```
#include "stdio.h"

#define MC68K

main ()
{
#ifdef MC68K
    printf ("compile Motorola version\n");
    /* statements here compiled for
       MC680X0 chip    */
       .
       .

#else
    printf ("compile Intel version\n");
    /* statements here compiled for Intel
       80X86 chip */
       .
```

```
#endif
#ifndef NATSEMI
    printf ("compile for Nat Semi chip
        too\n");
#endif
}
```

This kind of conditional compilation is widely used by software development organisations which have to produce versions of software for different markets, in this case different computers using popular microprocessors.

If MC68K is defined, the Motorola-specific code is compiled; if not, the Intel version is produced. NAT-SEMI is not defined; as a result of the '#ifndef', its version is compiled also.

Note that '#else' may be used with '#ifdef' and '#ifndef', but '#elif' may not be. '#endif' is necessary as a terminator to all '#if', '#ifdef' and '#ifndef' directives.

The preprocessor can be a useful debugging tool:

```
#define DEBUG
/* program code */
        .
        .
#ifdef DEBUG
    printf ("Debug information\n")
    /* print more debug information */
#endif
```

In a typical large program, there might be several hundred debug statements embedded. They only need to be removed when the program has become stable and correct. As soon as they are taken out, the program will fail of course. With the approach shown above, only one line need be deleted:

```
#define DEBUG
```

This 'switches off' all debug code. If the debug code is subsequently needed, the definition of DEBUG is re-introduced.

### #if and #elif

'#if' and '#elif' are similar to the foregoing, but actually test the value of the symbolic constant that has been defined with #define. For example:

```
#define DEBUG 2
      .
      .
/* program code  */
      .
      .
#if DEBUG == 1
    /* debug level 1 */
#elif DEBUG == 2
    /* debug level 2 */
#elif DEBUG == 3
    /* debug level 3 */
#else
    printf ("No debugging\n");
#endif
```

Here, only the value of DEBUG has to be changed to decide which code is compiled.

### #undef and #define

The '#undef' directive causes a previously-defined name to be 'forgotten' by the preprocessor. To redefine the name requires use of the '#define' directive with that name.

'#define' may be used for simple arithmetic:

```
#define ONE    1
#define TWO    ONE + ONE
```

This is correct, causing substitution of '1' by the preprocessor for both instances of 'ONE' in the second line. The preprocessor's method of substitution causes the next line to fail:

```
#define FOUR   TWO * TWO
```

Here, the value of TWO – the pattern '1 + 1' – is multiplied by itself, giving 3 and not, as expected, four.

The '#define' directive may be used to define preprocessor macros, which are analogous to functions. If there is no white space between a defined symbolic constant and a following left parenthesis, that symbolic constant is treated as such a macro. For example:

```
#define getchar() getc(stdin)
```

This is a good example, from 'stdio.h', of the definition of the 'getchar' macro.

Care needs to be taken with variables in macros written using '#define'. Here is an example:

```
#define MIN(a,b) ((a) < (b) ? (a) : (b))
```

This is called from program code and works fine for simple operands. Problems arise when operands are used which change their own values. If this is tried:

```
MIN (x++, 14);
```

and if x has an initial value of 11, the macro is expanded like this:

```
((11) < (14) ? (12) : (14))
```

This causes 12 to be reported as the minimum, not 11.

### #include
'#include' causes header files to be included in the form of their full source code in the program source code. Two usages are possible:

```
#include "header.h"
```

and

```
#include <header.h>
```

The first form searches in the system's standard directories for holding header files and in the user's own directory; the version with angle brackets does not search in the user's directory.

Finally, it should be noted that header files may be nested to arbitrary depth and that definitions made with '#define' may contain other definitions.

Such nesting is sometimes useful, but it should never be made too complex, as any programmer will know who has ever had to search down five levels of '#include' files to find out if a variable is an 'int' or a 'char'!

**Other directives, operators and macros**

The remaining preprocessor directives, operators and macros are relatively little-used; some are new with the ANSI standard.

ANSI C specifies the unary '#' (*stringization*) and '##' (*token merging*) operators.

Consider the following macro definition:

```
#define makeexe(filename) #filename ".exe"
```

and the subsequent macro call:

```
makeexe(myprog)
```

The resulting value of `filename` is the string `"myprog.exe"`.

Here is an example of token-merging:

```
#define mystrcat(s1, s2) s1 ## s2
```

This results in the concatenation of the input strings `s1` and `s2`.

The ANSI standard also specifies the following preprocessor macro names:

```
__LINE__
__FILE__
__DATE__
__TIME__
__STDC__
```

- '__LINE__' contains a decimal value corresponding to the currently-compiling source code line in the program.

- '__FILE__' is a pointer to a string which is the name of the source file.

- '__DATE__' is the date of translation given as a string in the style `"Sep 25 yyyy"`.

- '__TIME__' is the time of translation given as a string in the style `"hh:mm:ss"`.

- '__STDC__' is set to the integer constant 1 if and only if the compiler conforms to the ANSI standard.

These macros might be used like this:

```
fprintf(stderr,"Program error line %d
    file %s at time %s\n", __LINE__,
    __FILE__, __TIME__);
```

The '#line' directive is used rarely, usually for production of diagnostic messages and by programs that generate C source code as output. The directive is of the form:

```
#line <number> <filename>
```

or

```
#line <number>
```

The directive indicates that the next source code line is derived from line <number> of an original source code file called <filename> or, for the second form, the last <filename> mentioned in a '#line' directive. The '#line' directive is most often used to set the value of the '__LINE__' macro.

The '#error' directive causes the compiler to stop when it is encountered and optionally prints a diagnostic message:

```
#error Halted for debugging.
```

'#pragma' is an implementation-defined directive which allows various instructions to be given to the compiler:

```
#pragma <pname>
```

where the token-sequence <pname> contains the instructions.

## 10.3 Bit twiddling

The elements of bit-manipulation operations using the bitwise operators were introduced in Chapter 4. To recap, here is the set of bitwise operators:

| & | bitwise AND |
|---|---|
| \| | bitwise OR |
| ^ | bitwise exclusive OR |
| ~ | one's complement |
| >> | right bit shift |
| << | left bit shift |

Bit operations may only be done on integer data types.

As in Chapter 4, we use a variable called state_flag and treat it as if it were eight bits long. We assume that the initial value of state_flag is:

```
00001010
```

where the leftmost bit is number 7 and the rightmost is numbered zero.

We also define four symbolic constants as 'masks':

```
#define   DEV_TX    1
#define   DEV_RX    2
#define   DEV_WAIT  4
#define   BUF_FULL  8
```

The bitwise AND operator '&' is used to find if bits are switched on (value 1) and to switch bits off. For example:

```
if (state_flag & BUF_FULL)
```

This checks whether bit 3 is set indicating the receiving buffer is full. Bit 3 is set, so a non-zero (TRUE) value is returned. Bit 3 might be 'switched off' like this:

```
state_flag &= 0xF7;   /* Binary 11110111 */
```

The value of bit 3 is ANDed with the lone zero in the mask and therefore 'switched off'; any other 1 values in state_flag are left intact.

The bitwise OR operator '|' is used to set bits on:

```
state_flag |= DEV_WAIT;
```

This sets bit 2 on, to indicate that the communications device is in a wait state.

The one's complement operator flips all the bits in its operand:

```
state_flag = ~state_flag;
```

This changes the value of state_flag from its initial

```
00001010
```

to

```
11110101
```

This leads to a foolproof way of switching off bits in combination with the '&' operator:

```
state_flag = state_flag & ~DEV_WAIT;
```

The mask 0xF7 used above to switch off bit 3 assumes that state_flag is eight bits long; if there are any 1-bits to the left of the eight, it will inadvertently switch them off.

The combination of operators is more portable than other methods of switching off bits, since it does not assume any particular size of integer as its operand but ensures that all bits to the left of the one being set off will be unchanged.

The exclusive-or operator '^' can be used to reverse bit values:

```
state_flag ^= 0x7;
```

This flips the values of bits 0, 1 and 2.

The left-shift operator '<<' shifts the bits in its first operand to the left by the number of places specified by its second operand. Left-shifting is equivalent to multiplication of the operand by 2.

The right-shift operator '>>' shifts the bits in its first operand to the right by the number of places specified by its second operand. Right-shifting is equivalent to integer division by 2 of the operand.

Finally, the bit field `state_flag` may be usefully printed in octal or hexadecimal using the 'printf' format codes `%o` and `%x`. The result makes it easier to read the values of the individual bits.

![section divider]

## Find the error

In each of the programs below, identify the line containing the error. Answers are given in Appendix C.

```
1    1   #include "stdio.h"
     2
     3   #define IX86
     4
     5   main()
     6   {
     7   #ifdef IX86
     8       printf ("Compile Intel version\n");
     9   #elif
     10      printf ("Compile Motorola
                                     version\n");
     11  #endif
     12  }


2    1   #define   DEV_TX    1
     2   #define   DEV_RX    2
     3   #define   DEV_WAIT  4
     4   #define   BUF_FULL  8
     5
     6   main ()
     7   {
     8       int state_flag;
     9
     10      /* Switch off wait bit */
     11
     12      state_flag = state_flag &&
                     ~DEV_WAIT;
     13  }
```

# Appendix A
# C library functions

The following is a list, in alphabetic order by function name, of C library functions included in the ANSI standard and declared in the standard header files:

'stdio.h'
'string.h'
'ctype.h'
'math.h'
'stdlib.h'

For the functions declared in 'math.h', there is a macro, also defined in 'math.h', called HUGE_VAL. If any of the 'math.h functions produces a value which is too large to be stored in a variable of type 'double', HUGE_VAL is returned, signifying a 'range error'. If the input to any of the 'math.h' functions is not in the required domain, a 'domain error' is the result; the function return value is implementation-dependent.

```
#include "stdlib.h"
void abort (void)
```

'abort' causes abnormal program termination.

```
#include "stdlib.h"
int abs (int num);
```

'abs' returns the absolute value of the integer num.

```
#include "math.h"
double acos (double x)
```

'acos' returns the arccosine of x in the range zero to PI.

```
#include "math.h"
double asin (double x)
```

'asin' returns the arcsine of x in the range -PI/2 to PI/2.

```
#include "math.h"
double atan (double x)
```

'atan' returns the arctangent of x in the range -PI/2 to PI/2.

```
#include "math.h"
double atan2 (double y, double x)
```

'atan2' returns the arctangent of y/x in the range -PI to PI, using the signs of both arguments to determine the quadrant of the return value.

```
#include "stdlib.h"
int atexit (void (*f) (void))
```

'atexit' causes the function 'f' to be called if the program terminates normally and returns non-zero if the function cannot be called.

```
#include "stdlib.h"
double atof (const char *s)
```

'atof' converts and returns as a double floating point number the string at s, returning zero on error.

```
#include "stdlib.h"
int atoi (const char *s)
```

'atoi' converts and returns as an integer the string at s, returning zero on error.

```
#include "stdlib.h"
int atol (const char *s)
```

'atol' converts and returns as a long integer the string at s, returning zero on error.

```
#include "stdlib.h"
void *bsearch (const void *key, const void
  *base, size_t n, size_t size,
  int (*comp)(const void *key, const void
  *element))
```

'bsearch' does a binary search on the sorted array pointed to by base and returns a pointer to the first member of the array which matches key. The number of array elements is specified by n and the size in bytes of each element by size. The type 'size_t' is defined as 'unsigned int' in 'stddef.h'. The function 'comp' compares array elements in turn with key. If key is not matched in the search, NULL is returned.

```
#include "stdlib.h"
void *calloc (size_t n, size_t size)
```

'calloc' allocates space in memory for n objects, each of size (in bytes) of size. The function returns a pointer to the allocated memory, or NULL if the memory could not be allocated.

```
#include "math.h"
double ceil (double x)
```

'ceil' returns the smallest integer, represented as a 'double', which is not less than x.

```
#include "stdio.h"
void clearerr (FILE *fp)
```

'clearerr' clears end-of-file and error status indicators for the file pointed to by fp.

```
#include "math.h"
double cos (double x)
```

'cos' returns the cosine of x in radians.

```
#include "math.h"
double cosh (double x)
```

'cosh' returns the hyperbolic cosine of x.

```
#include "stdlib.h"
div_t div (int n, int d)
```

'div' calculates the quotient and remainder of n/d. The results are stored in the 'int' members quot and rem of a structure of type 'div_t'. The type 'div_t' is defined in 'stdlib.h'.

```
#include "stdlib.h"
void exit (int status)
```

'exit' causes immediate normal program termination. The value of status is returned to the operating system environment. Zero status is treated as indicating normal termination.

```
#include "math.h"
double exp (double x)
```

'exp' returns the value of 'e' raised to the power of x.

```
#include "math.h"
double fabs (double x)
```

'fabs' returns the absolute value of x.

```
#include "stdio.h"
int fclose (FILE *fp)
```

'fclose' discards any buffered input or output for the file pointed to by fp and then closes the file. The function returns zero for successful file closure or EOF on error.

```
#include "stdio.h"
int feof (FILE *fp)
```

'feof' returns non-zero if the end of the file pointed to by fp has been reached; otherwise zero is returned.

```
#include "stdio.h"
int ferror (FILE *fp)
```

'ferror' checks if a file operation has produced an error. It returns non-zero if an error occurred during the last operation on the file pointed to by fp, zero otherwise.

```
#include "stdio.h"
int fflush (FILE *fp)
```

'fflush' causes the contents of any buffered but unwritten data to be written to the file pointed to by fp. The function returns zero if successful, EOF on failure.

```
#include "stdio.h"
int fgetc (FILE *fp)
```

'fgetc' returns the next character from the file pointed to by fp. It returns EOF on error or end-of-file.

```
#include "stdio.h"
int fgetpos (FILE *fp, fpos_t *ptr)
```

'fgetpos' stores in the pointer ptr the current position in the file pointed to by fp. The type 'fpos_t' is defined in 'stdio.h'. The function returns non-zero on error.

```
#include "stdio.h"
char *fgets (char *s, int n, FILE *fp)
```

'fgets' reads a string from the file pointed to by fp until a newline character is encountered or n - 1 characters have been read. If a newline is encountered it is included in the string s which is in any event null-terminated. The function returns s, or NULL on end-of-file or error.

```
#include "math.h"
double floor (double x)
```

'floor' returns the largest integer, represented as a 'double', which is not greater then x.

---

```
#include "math.h"
double fmod (double x, double y)
```

'fmod' returns the remainder of the division of x by y. If y is zero, the result is undefined.

---

```
#include "stdio.h"
FILE *fopen (const char *s, const char *mode)
```

'fopen' opens the file named in the string s in accordance with the open mode specified in the string mode. Legal modes are "r", "w" and "a" for reading, writing and appending; any of these suffixed with a '+' additionally opens the file for reading and writing. If a 'b' is suffixed to the mode string a binary file is indicated. 'fopen' returns a pointer to the file opened or NULL on error.

---

```
#include "stdio.h"
int fprintf (FILE *fp, const char *<format>,
  <varlist>)
```

'fprintf' is the same as 'printf', given below, except that its output is written to the file pointed to by fp.

---

```
#include "stdio.h"
int fputc (int c, FILE *fp)
```

'fputc' writes the character c to the file pointed to by fp. It returns c, or EOF on error. Although c is defined as an integer, it is treated as an 'unsigned char' in that only the low-order byte is used.

```
#include "stdio.h"
int fputs (const char *s, FILE *fp)
```

'fputs' writes the string s to the file pointed to by fp. The function returns a non-negative number, or EOF on error.

```
#include "stdio.h"
size_t fread (void *buf, size_t n,
  size_t count, FILE *fp)
```

'fread' reads, from the file pointed to by fp into the array at buf, up to count objects of size n. The function returns the number of objects read.

```
#include "stdlib.h"
void free (void *p)
```

'free' de-allocates the memory pointed to by p and makes it available for other use. Before 'free' is called, memory must have been allocated and p initialised by one of the library functions 'malloc', 'calloc' or 'realloc'.

```
#include "stdio.h"
FILE *freopen (const char *s, const char
  *mode, FILE *fp)
```

'freopen' opens the file named in the string s and associates with it the file pointer fp. The function returns that file pointer or NULL on error.

```
#include "math.h"
double frexp (double x, int *exp)
```

'frexp' returns x in two parts: a fraction between 0.5 and 1 in x, and a power of two at the integer pointer exp. If x is initially zero, the returned parameters are also both zero.

```
#include "stdio.h"
int fscanf (FILE *fp, const char *<format>,
  <varlist>)
```

'fscanf' is the same as 'scanf', given below, except that the input is read from the file pointed to by fp.

```
#include "stdio.h"
int fseek (FILE *fp, long n, int origin)
```

'fseek' is usually used with binary streams. When so used, it causes the file position for the file pointed to by fp to be set to a displacement of n characters from `origin`. `origin` may be any of three macro values defined in 'stdio.h': SEEK_SET (start of file), SEEK_CUR (current position in file) or SEEK_END (end-of-file). Used with text streams, n must be zero, or a return value from 'ftell' with `origin` set to SEEK_SET. The function returns non-zero on error.

```
#include "stdio.h"
int fsetpos (FILE *fp, const fpos_t *ptr)
```

'fsetpos' returns the position of fp to the position stored by 'fgetpos' in `ptr`. The function returns non-zero on error.

```
#include "stdio.h"
long ftell (FILE *fp)
```

'ftell' returns the current file position for the file pointed to by fp, or returns -1 on error.

```
#include "stdio.h"
size_t fwrite (void *buf, size_t n,
  size_t count, FILE *fp)
```

'fwrite' causes count objects of size n bytes to be written from buf to the file pointed to by fp and returns the number of such objects written. A number less than count is returned on error.

```
#include "stdio.h"
int getc (FILE *fp)
```

'getc' reads the next character from the file pointed to by fp and returns it, or EOF on end-of-file or error. 'getc' is a macro and is equivalent to 'fgetc', given above.

```
#include "stdio.h"
int getchar (void)
```

'getchar' reads the next character from standard input and returns that character, or EOF on end-of-file or error. 'getchar ()' is the same as 'getc (stdin)'.

```
#include "stdlib.h"
char *getenv (const char *s)
```

'getenv' returns the operating-system environment string associated with the identifier named in the string at s. Further details are system-dependent.

```
#include "stdio.h"
char *gets (char *s)
```

'gets' reads from standard input an input line into the array at s, replacing the terminating newline with a null terminator. The string s is also returned by 'gets', or NULL on end-of-file or error.

```
#include "ctype.h"
int isalnum (int c)
```

'isalnum' returns non-zero if c is alphanumeric, zero otherwise.

```
#include "ctype.h"
int isalpha (int c)
```

'isalpha' returns non-zero if c is alphabetic, zero otherwise.

```
#include "ctype.h"
int iscntrl (int c)
```

'iscntrl' returns non-zero if c is a control character (0 to 037, or DEL (0177), in the ASCII set), zero otherwise.

```
#include "ctype.h"
int isdigit (int c)
```

'isdigit' returns non-zero if c is a digit, zero otherwise.

```
#include "ctype.h"
int isgraph (int c)
```

'isgraph' returns non-zero if c is a printable character other than a space, zero otherwise.

```
#include "ctype.h"
int islower (int c)
```

'islower' returns non-zero if c is a lowercase letter in the range 'a' to 'z', zero otherwise.

```
#include "ctype.h"
int isprint (int c)
```

'isprint' returns non-zero if c is a printable character including space, zero otherwise.

```
#include "ctype.h"
int ispunct (int c)
```

'ispunct' returns non-zero if c is a printable character other than space, letter and digit, zero otherwise.

```
#include "ctype.h"
int isspace (int c)
```

'isspace' returns non-zero if c is any of space, tab, vertical tab, carriage return, newline or formfeed, zero otherwise.

```
#include "ctype.h"
int isupper (int c)
```

'isupper' returns non-zero if c is an upper-case letter in the range 'A' to 'Z', zero otherwise.

```
#include "ctype.h"
int isxdigit (int c)
```

'isxdigit' returns non-zero if c is a hexadecimal digit in the range 'a' to 'f', 'A' to 'F', or 0 to 9, zero otherwise.

```
#include "stdlib.h"
long labs (long n)
```

'labs' returns as a long integer the absolute value of the long integer n.

```
#include "math.h"
double ldexp (double x, int n)
```

'ldexp' returns as a double floating-point number the result of x * (2 ** n).

```
#include "stdlib.h"
ldiv_t ldiv (int n, int d)
```

'ldiv' calculates the quotient and remainder of n/d. The results are stored in the 'long' members quot and rem of a structure of type 'ldiv_t'. The type 'ldiv_t' is defined in 'stdlib.h'.

```
#include "math.h"
double log (double x)
```

'log' returns as a double floating-point number the natural logarithm of x.

```
#include "math.h"
double log10 (double x)
```

'log10' returns as a double floating-point number the logarithm to base 10 of x.

```
#include "stdlib.h"
void *malloc (size_t size)
```

'malloc' allocates space in memory for an object with size (in bytes) of size. The function returns a pointer to the allocated memory, or NULL if the memory could not be allocated.

```
#include "string.h"
void *memchr (const void *s, unsigned char
  c, size_t n)
```

'memchr' returns a pointer to the first occurrence of the character c within the first n characters of the array s. The function returns NULL if there is no match. The type 'size_t' is defined in 'stddef.h' as an unsigned integer.

```
#include "string.h"
int memcmp (const void *s1, const void *s2,
  size_t n)
```

'memcmp' compares the first n characters of s1 with those of s2 and returns an integer less than, equal to or greater than zero depending on whether s1 is lexicographically less than, equal to or greater than s2.

```
#include "string.h"
void *memcpy (void *outs, const void *ins,
  size_t n)
```

'memcpy' causes n characters to be copied from the array ins to the array outs. The function returns a pointer to outs.

```
#include "string.h"
void *memmove (void *outs, const void *ins,
  size_t n)
```

'memmove' causes n characters to be copied from the array ins to the array outs, additionally allowing the copy to take place even if the objects being copied overlap in memory. The function returns a pointer to outs.

```
#include "string.h"
void *memset(void *s, unsigned char c,
  size_t n)
```

'memset' causes the first n characters of the array s to be filled with the character c. The function returns a pointer to s.

---

```
#include "math.h"
double modf (double x, double *iptr)
```

'modf' returns the integral part of x at the 'double' pointer iptr. The function returns the fractional part of x.

---

```
#include "stdio.h"
void perror (const char *s)
```

'perror' prints to the standard error device the string s, followed by an error message generated according to the contents of the value of the variable errno, defined in 'errno.h'.

---

```
#include "math.h"
double pow (double x, double y)
```

'pow' returns as a double floating-point number the value of x raised to the power of y.

---

```
#include "stdio.h"
int printf (const char *<format>, <varlist>)
```

'printf' writes to standard output the contents of the format string, other than special control sequences contained in the format string, followed by the contents of a list of variables converted according to the control sequences in the format string. These are the 'printf' format codes and their meanings:

d, i, o, u   The variable corresponding to the
x, X         format code is converted to decimal
(d,i), octal (o), unsigned decimal (u) or unsigned hexadecimal (x and X). The x conversion uses the letters abcdef; X uses ABCDEF.

The format string can specify a minimum width for any field by specifying a decimal number after the '%'.

f       The variable is converted to a decimal notation of form [-]ddd.ddd, where the minimum width (w) of the field and the precision (p) are specified by %w.pf. The default precision is 6 characters; a precision of zero causes the decimal point to be suppressed.

e, E    The float or double variable is converted to 'scientific notation' of form [-]d.ddde±dd. Width and precision may also be specified. The default precision is 6 characters; a precision of zero causes the decimal point to be suppressed.

g, G    The float or double variable is printed in style 'f' or 'e'. Style 'e' is used only if the exponent resulting from the conversion is less than -4 or greater than or equal to the precision. Trailing zeroes are removed. A decimal point appears only if it is followed by a digit.

c       The variable is printed as a character.

s       The variable is taken to be a string (character pointer) and characters from the string are printed until a null character is encountered or the number of characters indicated by the precision specification is reached.

P       Print variable as a pointer of type 'void *'.

n       The associated variable is a pointer to an integer which is assigned the number of characters written so far by 'printf' on this call.

%       Print a '%'.

A range of modifiers may be used with the format codes to specify the field width, signing and justification, precision and length of the converted output.

An integer between the percent sign and the format code specifies the minimum width of the output field. The output is padded, if necessary, with spaces, or with zeros if the integer is prefixed with a '0'.

All output is, by default, right-justified; it can be left-justified by insertion of a '-' before the format code (and minimum width specifier, if any). Similar insertion of a '+' ensures the number is printed with a sign; a space character causes a space to prefix the output if there is no sign.

Precision is specified if the minimum width specifier is followed by a full-stop and an integer. The value of the integer specifies the maximum number of characters to be printed from a string, or the minimum number of digits to be printed for an integer, or the number of decimal places to be printed, or the number of significant digits for output of floating-point data.

Length modifiers 'h', 'l' and 'L' are available. 'h' causes the corresponding variable to be printed as a 'short'; 'l' as a 'long' and 'L' as a 'long double'.

---

```
#include "stdio.h"
int putc (int c, FILE *fp)
```

'putc' writes the character c to the file pointed to by fp and returns it; it returns EOF on error. 'putc' is a macro and is equivalent to 'fputc', given above.

---

```
#include "stdio.h"
int putchar (int c)
```

'putchar' writes the next character to standard output and returns that character, or EOF on error. 'putchar (c)' is the same as 'putc (c, stdout)'.

```
#include "stdio.h"
int puts (const char *s)
```

'puts' writes the string s to the standard output, followed by a newline. The function returns EOF on error, otherwise a zero or positive number.

```
#include "stdlib.h"
void qsort (void *base, size_t n, size_t
  size, int (*comp)(const void *key, const
  void *element))
```

'qsort' sorts the array pointed to by base, which contains n elements of size size, using the recursive Quicksort algorithm. The function 'comp' compares array elements in turn with key and returns a negative, zero or positive integer depending on whether key is less than, equal to or greater than element.

```
#include "stdlib.h"
int rand (void)
```

'rand' returns a (pseudo) random number in the range zero to at least 32,767.

```
#include "stdlib.h"
void *realloc (void *ptr, size_t size)
```

'realloc' changes the size in memory for the object pointed to by ptr to size. The function returns a pointer to the re-allocated memory, or NULL if the memory could not be re-allocated. If NULL is returned, the value of ptr is unchanged.

```
#include "stdio.h"
int remove (const char *s)
```

'remove' erases the file named in the string s, returning zero on success, non-zero on error.

```
#include "stdio.h"
int rename (const char *s1, const char *s2)
```

'rename' changes the name of the file named in string s1 to the name in s2, returning zero on success, non-zero on error.

```
#include "stdio.h"
void rewind (FILE *fp)
```

'rewind' resets the file position indicator to the beginning of the file pointed to by fp.

```
#include "stdio.h"
int scanf (const char *<format>, <varlist>)
```

'scanf' reads from the standard input data which is converted and stored in memory at the addresses specified by a number of pointer variables in the variable list. Conversions are performed according to the format string specifications corresponding to the individual variables. Ordinary (non-format specifier) characters in the format string must correspond to the next non-whitespace character of input. These are the 'scanf' format codes:

| | |
|---|---|
| d, i, o, u, x | Read a decimal, integer, octal, unsigned or hexadecimal number from standard input and place at an integer pointer specified in the argument list. |
| e, f, g | Read a floating-point number and place at a 'float' pointer specified in the argument list. |
| c, s | Read: (c) a number of characters (default 1); (s) a string. In both cases place the input at a character pointer specified in the argument list. |
| p | Read a pointer (of type 'void *', as output by 'printf') and place at a pointer specified in the argument list. |

| | |
|---|---|
| [] | Read the longest string of input characters from the scan set between brackets and place at a character pointer specified in the argument list. A null terminator is added. |
| [^] | Read the longest set of input characters not from the scan set between brackets and place at a character pointer specified in the argument list. A null terminator is added. |
| % | Literal '%'; no assignment. |

A range of modifiers may be used with the format codes to suppress assignment of input and to specify maximum field length.

An asterisk '*' between the percent sign and the format code causes the input field corresponding to the format code to be discarded.

Maximum field width is specified by an integer after the '%' sign in the format string. Input characters effectively truncated by the maximum value will be stored at the next variable, if any, in the variable list.

Length modifiers 'h', 'l' and 'L' are available. 'h' causes the input to be stored at a pointer to a variable of type 'short'. 'l' causes input to be stored at a pointer to a variable of type 'long', or to modify the effect of the '%f', '%g' and '%e' specifiers so that the input is assigned to a pointer to a variable of type 'double'. 'L' causes input to be stored at a 'long double'.

---

```
#include "stdio.h"
void setbuf (FILE *fp, char *s)
```

'setbuf' sets the buffer for the file pointed to by fp to s; full buffering is specified. If s is NULL, buffering is turned off for the file.

```
#include "stdio.h"
int setvbuf (FILE *fp, char *s, int m,
  size_t size)
```

'setvbuf' allows different types of buffering to be specified for the file pointed to by fp. Symbolic-constant buffering modes, which are supplied as arguments to m, are defined in 'stdio.h'. _IOFBF, _IOLBF and _IONBF cause full, line and no buffering respectively. If s is not null, it is used as the file buffer, with buffer size determined by size. The function returns non-zero on error.

```
#include "math.h"
double sin (double x)
```

'sin' returns the sine of x in radians.

```
#include "math.h"
double sinh (double x)
```

'sinh' returns the hyperbolic sine of x.

```
#include "stdio.h"
int sprintf (char *s, const char *<format>,
  <varlist>)
```

'sprintf' is the same as 'printf', given above, except that its output is written to the string pointed to by s, which is null-terminated.

```
#include "math.h"
double sqrt (double x)
```

'sqrt' returns the non-negative square root of x; the value of x must not be negative.

```
#include "stdlib.h"
void srand (unsigned int seed)
```

'srand' generates a new set of (pseudo) random numbers using seed, which has an initial value of 1, as the seed.

```
#include "stdio.h"
int sscanf (char *s, const char *<format>,
  <varlist>)
```

'sscanf' is the same as 'scanf', given above, except
that the input is read from the string pointed to by
s.

---

```
#include "string.h"
char *strcat (char *s1, const char *s2)
```

'strcat' appends a copy of string s2 to the end of s1
and returns a pointer to the null-terminated result.

---

```
#include "string.h"
char *strchr (const char *s, int c)
```

'strchr' returns a pointer to the first occurrence of
character c in string s or a NULL pointer if c does
not occur in s.

---

```
#include "string.h"
int strcmp (const char *s1, const char *s2)
```

'strcmp' compares its arguments and returns an integer less than, equal to or greater than zero
depending on whether s1 is lexicographically less
than, equal to or greater than s2.

---

```
#include "string.h"
char *strcpy(char *s1, const char *s2)
```

'strcpy' copies string s2 to s1, stopping after the
null character has been copied and returning a
pointer to s1.

---

```
#include "string.h"
size_t strcspn (const char *s1, const char *s2)
```

'strcspn' returns the length of the initial segment of
the string s1 which consists entirely of characters
not in s2.

```
#include "string.h"
char *strerror (size_t n)
```

'strerror' returns a pointer to a string corresponding to a system-dependent error number n.

---

```
#include "string.h"
size_t strlen (const char *s)
```

'strlen' returns the number of characters in s, not counting the null-terminator.

---

```
#include "string.h"
char *strncat (char *s1, const char *s2,
   int n)
```

'strncat' appends at most n characters from s2 to s1 and returns a pointer to the null-terminated result.

---

```
#include "string.h"
int strncmp (const char *s1, const char *s2,
   int n)
```

'strncmp' is the same as 'strcmp', but compares at most n characters.

---

```
#include "string.h"
char *strncpy (char *s1, const char *s2,
   int n)
```

'strncpy' copies exactly n characters, truncating s2 or adding null characters to s1 if necessary. The result is not null-terminated if the length of s2 is n or more. A pointer to s1 is returned.

---

```
#include "string.h"
char *strpbrk (const char * s1, const char
   *s2)
```

'strpbrk' returns a pointer to the first occurrence in string s1 of any character from string s2, or a NULL character if there is no match.

```
#include "string.h"
char *strrchr (const char *s, int c)
```

'strrchr' is the same as 'strchr' except that a pointer to the last occurrence of the character in the string is returned.

---

```
#include "string.h"
size_t strspn (const char *s1, const char *s2)
```

'strspn' returns the length of the initial segment of s1 which consists entirely of characters from s2.

---

```
#include "string.h"
char *strstr (const char *s1, const char *s2)
```

'strstr' returns a pointer to the first occurrence of s2 in s1, or NULL if there is no match.

---

```
#include "stdlib.h"
double strtod (const char *s, char **ptr)
```

'strtod' returns as a double floating-point number the value represented by the character string pointed to by s. An optional string of white space characters, an optional sign, a string of digits optionally containing a decimal point, and an optional 'e' or 'E' followed by an optional sign are recognised by 'strtod'. 'strtod' scans the input string up to the first unrecognised character; if the contents of ptr are not NULL, a pointer to the character terminating the scan is stored in *ptr.

'atof (s)' is equivalent to 'strtod (s, (char **)0)'

---

```
#include "string.h"
char *strtok (char *s1, const char *s2)
```

'strtok' considers the string s1 to consist of a sequence of zero or more text tokens separated by spans of one or more characters from the separator string s2. The function is called iteratively, returning pointers to tokens extracted from s1 and delimited by a character from s2. 'strtok' returns NULL when it finds no further tokens.

```
#include "stdlib.h"
long strtol (const char *s, char **ptr, int
  base)
```

'strtol' returns as a long integer the value represented by the character string pointed to by s. Leading white space is ignored. The string is scanned up to the first character inconsistent with the base. If the contents of ptr are not NULL, a pointer to the character terminating the scan is stored in *ptr. If no integer can be formed, that location is set to s and zero is returned. If base is zero, the base to be used is calculated automatically. Otherwise, the base must not be negative or greater than 36. Any overflow or underflow conditions cause a return value of LONG_MAX or LONG_MIN, defined in 'limits.h'.

---

```
#include "stdlib.h"
unsigned long strtoul (const char *s, char
  **ptr, int base)
```

'strtoul' is the same as 'strtol' except for its return type and its error return values of ULONG_MAX and ULONG_MIN.

---

```
#include "math.h"
double tan (double x)
```

'tan' returns the tangent of x in radians.

---

```
#include "math.h"
double tanh (double x)
```

'tanh' returns the hyperbolic tangent of x.

---

```
#include "stdio.h"
FILE *tmpfile (void)
```

'tmpfile' returns a pointer to a temporary file of access mode "wb+" which is automatically removed on closure. The function returns NULL on error.

```
#include "stdio.h"
char *tmpnam (char *s)
```

If s is NULL, 'tmpnam' generates a string which is not the name of an existing file and returns a pointer to an internal static array. If s is not NULL, the name string is additionally stored in s.

---

```
#include "ctype.h"
int tolower (int c)
```

'tolower' converts c to lower-case and returns c.

---

```
#include "ctype.h"
int toupper (int c)
```

'toupper' converts c to upper-case and returns c.

---

```
#include "stdio.h"
int ungetc (int c, FILE *fp)
```

'ungetc' returns the character c to the file pointed to by fp; c will be returned on the next read. The function returns the character returned or EOF on error.

---

```
#include "stdio.h"
int vfprintf (FILE *fp, const char
  *<format>, va_list arg)
```

'vfprintf' is the same as 'fprintf' except that arg is initialised with the argument list by the 'va_start' macro in 'stdarg.h'.

---

```
#include "stdio.h"
int vprintf (const char *<format>, va_list
  arg)
```

'vprintf' is the same as 'printf' except that arg is initialised with the argument list by the 'va_start' macro in 'stdarg.h'.

```
#include "stdio.h"
int vsprintf (char *s, const char *<format>,
  va_list arg)
```

'vsprintf' is the same as 'sprintf' except that arg is initialised with the argument list by the 'va_start' macro in 'stdarg.h'.

# Appendix B
# ASCII character set

A map of the ASCII character set is given below, with octal, decimal and hexadecimal numeric character representations.

## Octal map

| | | | | | | | |
|---|---|---|---|---|---|---|---|
| 000 nul | 001 soh | 002 stx | 003 etx | 004 eot | 005 enq | 006 ack | 007 bel |
| 010 bs | 011 ht | 012 nl | 013 vt | 014 np | 015 cr | 016 so | 017 si |
| 020 dle | 021 dc1 | 022 dc2 | 023 dc3 | 024 dc4 | 025 nak | 026 syn | 027 etb |
| 030 can | 031 em | 032 sub | 033 esc | 034 fs | 035 gs | 036 rs | 037 us |
| 040 sp | 041 ! | 042 " | 043 # | 044 $ | 045 % | 046 & | 047 ' |
| 050 ( | 051 ) | 052 * | 053 + | 054 , | 055 - | 056 . | 057 / |
| 060 0 | 061 1 | 062 2 | 063 3 | 064 4 | 065 5 | 066 6 | 067 7 |
| 070 8 | 071 9 | 072 : | 073 ; | 074 < | 075 = | 076 > | 077 ? |
| 100 @ | 101 A | 102 B | 103 C | 104 D | 105 E | 106 F | 107 G |
| 110 H | 111 I | 112 J | 113 K | 114 L | 115 M | 116 N | 117 O |
| 120 P | 121 Q | 122 R | 123 S | 124 T | 125 U | 126 V | 127 W |
| 130 X | 131 Y | 132 Z | 133 [ | 134 \ | 135 ] | 136 ^ | 137 _ |
| 140 ` | 141 a | 142 b | 143 c | 144 d | 145 e | 146 f | 147 g |
| 150 h | 151 i | 152 j | 153 k | 154 l | 155 m | 156 n | 157 o |
| 160 p | 161 q | 162 r | 163 s | 164 t | 165 u | 166 v | 167 w |
| 170 x | 171 y | 172 z | 173 { | 174 | | 175 } | 176 ~ | 177 del |

## Decimal map

| | | | | | | | |
|---|---|---|---|---|---|---|---|
| 00 nul | 01 soh | 02 stx | 03 etx | 04 eot | 05 enq | 06 ack | 07 bel |
| 08 bs | 09 ht | 10 nl | 11 vt | 12 np | 13 cr | 14 so | 15 si |
| 16 dle | 17 dc1 | 18 dc2 | 19 dc3 | 20 dc4 | 21 nak | 22 syn | 23 etb |
| 24 can | 25 em | 26 sub | 27 esc | 28 fs | 29 gs | 30 rs | 31 us |
| 32 sp | 33 ! | 34 " | 35 # | 36 $ | 37 % | 38 & | 39 ' |
| 40 ( | 41 ) | 42 * | 43 + | 44 , | 45 - | 46 . | 47 / |
| 48 0 | 49 1 | 50 2 | 51 3 | 52 4 | 53 5 | 54 6 | 55 7 |
| 56 8 | 57 9 | 58 : | 59 ; | 60 < | 61 = | 62 > | 63 ? |
| 64 @ | 65 A | 66 B | 67 C | 68 D | 69 E | 70 F | 71 G |
| 72 H | 73 I | 74 J | 75 K | 76 L | 77 M | 78 N | 79 O |
| 80 P | 81 Q | 82 R | 83 S | 84 T | 85 U | 86 V | 87 W |
| 88 X | 89 Y | 90 Z | 91 [ | 92 \ | 93 ] | 94 ^ | 95 _ |
| 96 ` | 97 a | 98 b | 99 c | 100 d | 101 e | 102 f | 103 g |
| 104 h | 105 i | 106 j | 107 k | 108 l | 109 m | 110 n | 111 o |
| 112 p | 113 q | 114 r | 115 s | 116 t | 117 u | 118 v | 119 w |
| 120 x | 121 y | 122 z | 123 { | 124 | | 125 } | 126 ~ | 127 del |

## Hexadecimal map

| | | | | | | | | | | | | | | | |
|---|---|---|---|---|---|---|---|---|---|---|---|---|---|---|---|
| 00 | nul | 01 | soh | 02 | stx | 03 | etx | 04 | eot | 05 | enq | 06 | ack | 07 | bel |
| 08 | bs | 09 | ht | 0a | nl | 0b | vt | 0c | np | 0d | cr | 0e | so | 0f | si |
| 10 | dle | 11 | dc1 | 12 | dc2 | 13 | dc3 | 14 | dc4 | 15 | nak | 16 | syn | 17 | etb |
| 18 | can | 19 | em | 1a | sub | 1b | esc | 1c | fs | 1d | gs | 1e | rs | 1f | us |
| 20 | sp | 21 | ! | 22 | " | 23 | # | 24 | $ | 25 | % | 26 | & | 27 | ' |
| 28 | ( | 29 | ) | 2a | * | 2b | + | 2c | , | 2d | - | 2e | . | 2f | / |
| 30 | 0 | 31 | 1 | 32 | 2 | 33 | 3 | 34 | 4 | 35 | 5 | 36 | 6 | 37 | 7 |
| 38 | 8 | 39 | 9 | 3a | : | 3b | ; | 3c | < | 3d | = | 3e | > | 3f | ? |
| 40 | @ | 41 | A | 42 | B | 43 | C | 44 | D | 45 | E | 46 | F | 47 | G |
| 48 | H | 49 | I | 4a | J | 4b | K | 4c | L | 4d | M | 4e | N | 4f | O |
| 50 | P | 51 | Q | 52 | R | 53 | S | 54 | T | 55 | U | 56 | V | 57 | W |
| 58 | X | 59 | Y | 5a | Z | 5b | [ | 5c | \ | 5d | ] | 5e | ^ | 5f | _ |
| 60 | ` | 61 | a | 62 | b | 63 | c | 64 | d | 65 | e | 66 | f | 67 | g |
| 68 | h | 69 | i | 6a | j | 6b | k | 6c | l | 6d | m | 6e | n | 6f | o |
| 70 | p | 71 | q | 72 | r | 73 | s | 74 | t | 75 | u | 76 | v | 77 | w |
| 78 | x | 79 | y | 7a | z | 7b | { | 7c | \| | 7d | } | 7e | ~ | 7f | del |

# Appendix C
# 'Find the Error' Answers


## Chapter 1

**1** Line 11: missing trailing double quote in 'printf'

**2** Line 9: space between trailing '*' and '/' in comment

**3** Line 12: missing terminating semi-colon

**4** Line 12: '%c' in 'printf' invalid format code for string

**5** Line 6: array subscript in range 1..100, should be 0..99

**6** Line 1: '#include' terminated with a semi-colon

**7** Line 11: unescaped double quotes embedded in 'printf'

**8** Line 5: condition in 'if' should have parentheses

**9** Line 4: superfluous '&' address operator in assignment

## Chapter 2

**1** Line 6: 'tax-all' is an invalid identifier; contains a hyphen

**2** Line 12: 'net_pay' defined 'const' and its value then changed

**3** Line 3: invalid type-specifier 'unsigned float'

**4** Line 1: reserved word 'switch' used as an identifier

**5** Line 3: variable c not initialised before comparison with EOF

**6** Line 12: invalid arithmetic on enumerated constant

## Chapter 3

**1** Line 19: 'do_net_pay' function header terminated with semi-colon

2 Line 19: type mismatch 'float tax_all' in function header

3 Line 3: 'float' return type missing from function declaration

4 Line 16: declarations follow statements in 'main'

5 Line 24: no return type in definition of function 'do_net_pay'

6 Lines 22 and 30: function nesting, 'do_net_pay' within 'main'

7 Line 27: net_pay only defined in 'main'; out of scope in 'do_net_pay'

8 Line 23: mismatched curly braces in 'main'

## Chapter 4

1 Line 9: precedence error in 'if': needs (x & MASK)

2 Line 11: invalid '+' on device: should be '++')

3 Line 11: invalid lvalue 'device++'

4 Line 6: comma operator forces s to be zeroed last; stg[s] is therefore garbage

## Chapter 5

1 Line 9: single '=' error in 'if'; should be '=='

2 Line 5: unbalanced parentheses in 'while' condition

3 Line 5: trailing semi-colon on 'while' condition

4 Line 14: 'goto' to label inside 'while' loop

5 Line 20: missing trailing semi-colon on 'do-while' condition

6 Line 27: 'goto' to label outside function containing 'goto'

7 Lines 8-14: all case labels must be constant expressions, not variables

## Chapter 6

1 Line 10: character pointer cptr not initialised

2 Line 3: too many initialisers (including null) for character array

3 Line 9: character array not null-terminated

4 Line 15: illegal array assignment – `outstring` not lvalue

5 Lines 10-11: array name rather than pointer name used in 'while' loop

## Chapter 7

1 Line 12: instance of structure not defined

2 Line 8: terminating semi-colon missing from structure declaration

3 Lines 20-28: pointer to structure members requires arrow operator

4 Line 12: pointer to structure not initialised

5 Line 8: structure declaration contains definition of itself

6 Line 13: type specified by 'typedef' wrongly used as structure name

7 Line 5: non-integer bit field member

## Chapter 8

1 Lines 3 and 9: string pointer `cptr` not initialised

2 Line 9: `cptr` in 'while' condition not de-referenced with '*'

3 Line 5: dangling reference; i destroyed on exit from the function; the pointer to i returned by the function 'f' points nowhere in the calling function

4 Lines 10 and 12: both instances of the pointer i in 'changei' must be de-referenced with '*'

5 Line 10: unbalanced parentheses in 'malloc' assignment

6 Line 5: 'fptr' is here defined as a function returning a pointer to an 'int'; to be a function pointer, (*fptr) should be used in all cases

7 Lines 8 and 11: mixed types and pointer arithmetic; `cptr` should be of type 'struct tnode*'

8 Line 12: attempt to increment array pointer by 'sizeof' structure type; only increment-by-one necessary

## Chapter 9

1  Line 19: output file opened in read mode

2  Lines 25-26: files not closed at end of program

3  Lines 9 and 11: 'scanf' requires pointers to its variable operands; the '&' operator is unnecessary with array operands

## Chapter 10

1  Line 9: '#elif' instead of '#else' used with '#ifdef'

2  Line 12: '&&' is not a bitwise operator; '&' must be used

# Index

# A

# B

# C

## G

## Q

## R